TOUCHDOWNS TO TAILGATING

THE RED BOOK
FOR ALL YOU NEED TO KNOW ABOUT
FOOTBALL AND HEINZ FIELD

BY CHARLES REICHBLUM
WITH RECIPES BY RANIA HARRIS

HEINZ FIELD TOUCHDOWNS TO TAILGATING

For information or inquires, address arpr, inc., 1420 Centre Avenue, Suite 2213, Pittsburgh, PA 15219 USA

ISBN: 0-9660991-9-2
Library of Congress Control Number: 2005931423

Printed in the United States of America, August, 2005 

TABLE OF CONTENTS

FOREWORD
A Message from H.J. Heinz Company

Dear Friends,

We enjoy watching football games at Heinz Field with our friends and families. These game-day celebrations regularly feature a wonderful array of foods. More often than not, we find ourselves talking about great sports traditions, the interesting features of Heinz Field, and the teams that call it home—the Pittsburgh Steelers and the University of Pittsburgh Panthers.

If you're like us, you'll agree that this book offers something for everyone. It pulls together interesting facts about Heinz Field and football, and offers up 57 terrific recipes using Heinz products. Special thanks to Chuck Reichblum and Rania Harris. They've given us a wonderful collection of football facts and tailgating tips.

But this book is much more. It's a special project to support the Western Pennsylvania Sports Museum. The museum pays tribute to Pittsburgh's incomparable sports history, and contributes to the quality of life in our region. Proceeds from the sale of each book help to fund future exhibits at the Sports Museum.

We hope you enjoy this book and savor its recipes. And, most of all, thank you for your contribution to the Western Pennsylvania Sports Museum.

With our gratitude,

Susie and Bill Johnson

William R. Johnson, *Chairman, President and CEO, with his wife, Susie*

PREFACE

As someone who has a great love and passion for western Pennsylvania's rich history and, now more than ever, its magnificent sports history, it's a wonderful honor to introduce you to this latest collection of information that brings together three of our region's very favorite things—Heinz, football and food!

In *Heinz Field Touchdowns to Tailgating*, raconteur extraordinaire Chuck Reichblum, a.k.a. "Dr. Knowledge," weaves together an inviting collection of tidbits, facts and secrets on the traditions of the H.J. Heinz Company—something we know quite a bit about at the Senator John Heinz Pittsburgh Regional History Center—Pittsburgh's beloved Steelers, and all things football. He then combines our love for Heinz and football with the best tailgating recipes ever from Pittsburgh's own Rania Harris—the perfect complement for your next football outing—at home or at Heinz Field.

I hope you enjoy the book and use it to make every Steelers game day an even more enjoyable experience! And thanks, too, for your purchase. Heinz is donating a portion of the proceeds to the History Center, which will continue to protect and chronicle the rich history that's been made and continues to be made in this wonderful western Pennsylvania area we call "home."

Andrew E. Masich
President & CEO
Senator John Heinz Pittsburgh Regional History Center
and Western Pennsylvania Sports Museum

CHAPTER 1

57 Q&As TO TEST YOUR FOOTBALL IQ

★ ★ ★ ★ ★

WHAT IS YOUR FOOTBALL IQ?

1. When the Steelers joined the NFL in 1933, they weren't called the Steelers. What was their original nickname?

2. When did the Steelers become the "Steelers"?

3. Since 1969, the Steelers have had only two head coaches—Chuck Noll and Bill Cowher. Who was the Steelers coach before Noll and Cowher started their long tenures?

4. Two men were head coaches of BOTH the Steelers and Pitt. Who were they?

5. In their history, the Steelers have had four different home fields. Can you name all four?

6. The Steelers have played three different opponents in the five Super Bowls they've been to. Which three teams have the Steelers played in the Super Bowls?

7. In the Steelers four Super Bowl wins, which players won the Most Valuable Player Award in each of those victories?

★ ★ ★ ★ ★

1. When the Steelers joined the NFL in 1933, their original nickname was the Pirates.

2. Pittsburgh's NFL team changed its nickname from Pirates to Steelers in 1940.

3. The Steelers head coach before Chuck Noll and Bill Cowher started their long tenures was Bill Austin. Austin coached the Steelers from 1966 through 1968.

4. The two men who coached both the Steelers and Pitt were Jock Sutherland and Johnny Michelosen.

5. The four home fields in Steelers history: Forbes Field, Pitt Stadium, Three Rivers Stadium and Heinz Field.

6. In the Steelers' five Super Bowl appearances, they've faced the Cowboys three times, the Vikings once, and the Rams once.

7. When the Steelers won their first Super Bowl in 1975, the MVP was Franco Harris. In the '76 Super Bowl, the MVP was Lynn Swann. In the 1979 and '80 Super Bowls, the MVP was Terry Bradshaw both times.

8. Has Pitt ever played in the Rose Bowl?

9. There are 12 major-college football teams whose nicknames do NOT end in "s." How many of these 12 can you name?

10. What are the most points ever scored by one team in an NFL game, whether regular or post-season game?

11. A football riddle: You can predict the score of any football game before it even starts and be right every time. How can you do that?

12. What are the most points ever scored by one team in a college football game?

★ ★ ★ ★ ★

8. Pitt has played in four Rose Bowl games—against Stanford in 1928, USC in 1930 and '33, and Washington in 1937.

9. The 12 major-college football teams whose nicknames don't end in "s": Alabama Crimson Tide, Illinois Fighting Illini, Marshall Thundering Herd, Navy Midshipmen, Nevada Wolf Pack, North Carolina State Wolfpack, North Texas Mean Green, Notre Dame Fighting Irish, Stanford Cardinal, Syracuse Orange, Tulane Green Wave and Tulsa Hurricane.

10. The most points ever scored by an NFL team in one game was 73, when the Chicago Bears beat the Washingon Redskins 73-0 in the championship game of 1940.

11. To predict the score of any football game before it even starts and be right every time, you can say, correctly, that the score of any game before it starts is always 0-0.

12. The record for most points scored by one team in a college football game was set in 1916 when Georgia Tech beat Cumberland 222-0.

WHAT IS YOUR FOOTBALL IQ?

13. When did a team that was not from any of the 50 U.S. states win the Super Bowl championship?

14. Besides the Steelers, five of today's NFL teams had different nicknames when they started—the Chicago Bears, Kansas City Chiefs, New York Jets, Tennessee Titans and Washington Redskins. What were these franchises' original nicknames?

15. Who were the three announcers during the first season of Monday Night Football on ABC?

16. Four U.S. Presidents played varsity college football. Do you know which four?

17. We all know a football field is 100 yards long from goal line to goal line, but how WIDE is a football field?

★ ★ ★ ★ ★

13. In 1983, '88 and '92, a team that was not from any of the 50 states won the Super Bowl. In those years, the Super Bowl was won by the Washington Redskins, whose stadium was then in the District of Columbia and not in any of the 50 U.S. states.

14. The Bears started as the Staleys (named for their sponsor, the Staley Starch Co.); the Chiefs were the Texans (then located in Dallas); the Jets were the Titans; the Titans were the Oilers; and the Redskins the Braves.

15. In ABC's first season of Monday Night Football in 1970, the announcers were Howard Cosell, Don Meredith and Keith Jackson.

16. The four U.S. Presidents who played varsity college football were Dwight Eisenhower at Army; Richard Nixon at Whittier College; Gerald Ford at Michigan; and Ronald Reagan at Eureka College.

17. A football field is 160 feet or 53-and-one-third yards wide.

18. Who was the only player to win the Heisman Trophy TWICE?

19. Which Pitt player won the Heisman?

20. Pitt has had three players who finished runners-up in the Heisman voting. Who are those three who came so close to winning the Heisman?

21. What man replaced his own father as head coach of an NFL team?

22. Why are the Green Bay Packers called "Packers"? How did they get that nickname?

18. The only player to win the Heisman Trophy twice was Archie Griffin of Ohio State. Griffin won it in both 1974 and '75.

19. Pitt's Heisman Trophy winner was Tony Dorsett in 1976.

20. The three Pitt players who finished runners-up in the Heisman voting were Larry Fitzgerald in 2003, Hugh Green in 1980, and Marshall Goldberg in 1938.

21. The man who replaced his father as head coach of an NFL team was Wade Phillips, who became head coach of the New Orleans Saints during the 1985 season. He replaced his father, Bum Phillips, who resigned.

22. The Green Bay Packers were originally financed by the Acme Packing Company of Green Bay, and because employees of that company were called "packers," they chose "Packers" as the team's name.

23. A son and his father were BOTH named Coach of the Year in college football the same year. Can you name them?

24. Which U.S. President played on a national championship team in college football?

25. When New York Jets quarterback Joe Namath famously "guaranteed" a victory over the Baltimore Colts in Super Bowl III, how many points underdog were the Jets in that game?

26. What team won the first football game ever played in America?

27. What player won the Heisman Trophy even though the team he played for LOST eight out of ten games that season?

★ ★ ★ ★ ★

23. Johnny Majors was voted Coach of the Year for major-college football in 1973 when he coached at Pitt, and his father, Shirley Majors, was voted Coach of the Year in small-college football for his coaching at Sewanee that same season.

24. U.S. President Gerald Ford was a center on the University of Michigan team that won the national championship in college football in 1933.

25. The Baltimore Colts were 17-point favorites to beat the New York Jets in Super Bowl III, but the Jets won, 16-7, fulfilling QB Joe Namath's prediction.

26. America's first football game was between Princeton and Rutgers in 1869. Football's first winner was Rutgers. They beat Princeton, 6-4.

27. Quarterback Paul Hornung of Notre Dame won the Heisman Trophy in 1956 even though his team won only two games that season and lost eight.

28. When was the first time a football game was televised, and which two teams played in that first TV game?

29. Who was the only athlete to play in both a Super Bowl and a World Series?

30. Has any head coach ever bettered Chuck Noll's record of winning four Super Bowls?

31. What former all-women's college is now a power in major-college football?

32. When did Pitt change its colors from blue & gold to red & white?

28. The first football game ever televised was Waynesburg College of Pennsylvania at Fordham University in New York. The game was played on Sept. 30, 1939, and televised in New York City.

29. The only athlete to play in both a Super Bowl and a World Series was Deion Sanders. Sanders played in Super Bowls with the 49ers and Cowboys, and in the World Series with the Braves.

30. Through 2005, Chuck Noll is the only head coach to win four Super Bowls.

31. Florida State was an all-women's college from 1901 until 1947, when they admitted men for the first time. Since then, their teams have become among the most successful in college football.

32. When Clark Shaughnessy was Pitt's football coach in 1943, he changed the team's colors to red & white because he had success with those colors as coach at Stanford. When Shaughnessy left Pitt after the 1945 season, the school went back to blue & gold.

33. Who are the only men to coach teams to the national championship in college football AS WELL AS the Super Bowl championship in Pro Football?

34. Who's the only Heisman Trophy winner ever to become a head coach in the NFL?

35. When was the last NFL game in which NEITHER team scored a point, and the game wound up with a final score of 0-0?

36. Which is the only team so far to have played in the Super Bowl FOUR straight years?

37. Who were the head coaches in the first Super Bowl game?

★ ★ ★ ★ ★

33. The only men to coach teams to the national championship in college football and to the Super Bowl championship in Pro Football are Jimmy Johnson (University of Miami and the Dallas Cowboys) and Barry Switzer (Oklahoma and the Dallas Cowboys).

34. The only Heisman Trophy winner to become a head coach in the NFL is Steve Spurrier, who won the Heisman at Florida and coached the Redskins in the NFL.

35. The last 0-0 game in the NFL was on Nov. 7, 1943, when the New York Giants and Detroit Lions played a scoreless game.

36. The only team to play in the Super Bowl four straight years is the Buffalo Bills, who played in Super Bowls XXV, XXVI, XXVII and XXVIII. (They lost all four).

37. Head coaches in the first Super Bowl game were Vince Lombardi of Green Bay and Hank Stram of Kansas City.

38. How can a team score a touchdown without crossing the goal line?

39. What father-son combination holds this record: The father quarterbacked an NFL team to Super Bowl titles, and his son quarterbacked a team to the national championship in college football?

40. Who was the first father-son combination to play in Super Bowl games?

41. Who was the first head coach of Pittsburgh's NFL team?

42. Four former Steelers head coaches are in the Pro Football Hall of Fame. Can you name all four?

38. A little-known rule allows a referee to award a team a touchdown for an "unfair act"—such as a player coming off the bench to tackle a runner headed for a TD. Thus, a team could score a touchdown without actually crossing the goal line.

39. Bob Griese quarterbacked Miami to two Super Bowl titles, in 1973 and 1974. His son, Brian, quarterbacked Michigan to the national championship in college football in 1997.

40. The first father-son combination to play in Super Bowl games was Tony Dorsett, who played in Super Bowls XII and XIII for Dallas, and his son, Anthony, who played in Super Bowl XXXIV with Tennessee.

41. The first head coach of Pittsburgh's NFL team was Forrest Douds. Douds coached the team in 1933 to a record of 3 wins, 6 losses and 2 ties.

42. The four Steelers head coaches in the Pro Football Hall of Fame are Chuck Noll, Walt Kiesling, Johnny Blood and Bert Bell.

WHAT IS YOUR FOOTBALL IQ?

43. One of college football's most famous backfields was the Pitt "Dream Backfield" of 1938. Can you name the four members of that backfield?

44. Who holds the all-time record for gaining the most yards rushing in Super Bowl history?

45. Which two NFL teams' nicknames are named after a real person?

46. Pittsburgh had Pro Football teams in two other leagues besides the NFL. What were those teams called, and what leagues were they in?

47. Who holds the record for playing Pro Football for the most years?

48. What are the most points ever scored by one player in one NFL game?

★ ★ ★ ★ ★

43. The four men in Pitt's "Dream Backfield" were Johnny Michelosen, Harold Stebbins, Dick Casiano and Marshall Goldberg.

44. The all-time rushing leader in Super Bowls is Franco Harris, who gained 354 yards in four games.

45. The Cleveland Browns are named after their first coach, Paul Brown. The Buffalo Bills' name came from William Cody, the showman and buffalo hunter known as Buffalo Bill.

46. The Pittsburgh Maulers played in the United States Football League in 1984, and the Pittsburgh Americans were in the American Football League in 1936 and '37.

47. The man who played the most years in Pro Football was quarterback-place kicker George Blanda. Blanda played for 26 seasons.

48. The most points scored by one player in an NFL game were 40, by Ernie Nevers of the Chicago Cardinals on Thanksgiving Day in 1929. Nevers scored six touchdowns and kicked four extra points.

WHAT IS YOUR FOOTBALL IQ?

49. Which major-college football team holds the record for winning the most games in a row?

50. What's the major-college record for most losses in a row?

51. What was the last college football team to go through an entire regular season and not allow any points to be scored against them all year?

52. Who was the youngest head coach ever to win the national championship in major-college football?

53. Of all the running backs in NFL history, which one led the league in rushing the most seasons?

54. The NFL once had teams named the Eskimos, Panhandles, Triangles, Yellow Jackets, Red Jackets, Steam Rollers and Gunners. In what cities did these teams play?

★ ★ ★ ★ ★

49. The major-college record for most victories in a row is held by Oklahoma. The Sooners won 47 consecutive games from 1953 to 1957.

50. Northwestern set the record for most losses in a row by a major-college team with 34 consecutive defeats from 1979 to 1982.

51. The last unscored-upon team in college football was Tennessee, in 1939. They shut out each of their 10 opponents during that regular season.

52. The youngest head coach ever to win the national championship in major-college football was Danny Ford, whose Clemson Tigers won the national championship in 1981 when Ford was 33 years old.

53. The running back who led the NFL in rushing for the most seasons was Jim Brown, who won the rushing title in eight different years.

54. Former NFL teams included the Duluth Eskimos, Columbus Panhandles, Dayton Triangles, Frankford Yellow Jackets, Minneapolis Red Jackets, Providence Steam Rollers and St. Louis Gunners.

55. Which stadium has hosted the most Super Bowls?

56. Who's the only man who was both the head coach of an NFL team AND the manager of a big league baseball team?

57. True or false? The Steelers once drafted William Shakespeare?

55. The stadium that's hosted the most Super Bowls is the New Orleans Superdome. Six Super Bowls have been played there.

56. Hugo Bezdek is the only man who managed a big league baseball team (the Pirates, 1917–19) and was head coach of an NFL team (Cleveland, 1937–38).

57. The Steelers drafted William Shakespeare, a back from Notre Dame, in the 1936 draft.

CHAPTER 2

57 AMAZING
FOOTBALL FUN FACTS

★ ★ ★ ★ ★

1. Can you imagine Bill Cowher, or any head coach of an NFL team, putting on a uniform, going out on the field, and being a regular player on his team?

That happened in the NFL in the early years—and the last time was with the Pittsburgh Steelers.

The Steelers head coach from 1937 to 1939 was Johnny Blood—and Blood was also a running and defensive back on his team.

Blood's record as a player-coach was 6-19—and it's never happened since.

2. Why are the Steelers the only team in the NFL that has their logo on only one side of their helmets?

The Steelers office gets more questions about this oddity than about anything else.

It all goes back to 1962 when the Steelers first decided to put a logo on their helmets. During that season, they wore gold helmets, and since they weren't sure how the logo would look on those helmets, equipment manager Jack Hart was instructed to put the logo on only one side—the right side—of the helmets. Team officials wanted to test the look before going all out.

In that 1962 season, the Steelers finished with a 9-5 record and became the winningest team in franchise history up to that time. They qualified for a post-season game and wanted to do something special for that game, so they changed the color of their helmets from gold to black—and that helped highlight the new logo.

Because of the interest generated by having the logo on only one side of their helmets, and because of the team's new success, the Steelers decided to leave it that way permanently, so today's helmet reflects the way the logo was originally applied and it's never been changed.

3.   Why does the Steelers logo look the way it does?

The logo is based on the Steelmark logo belonging to the American Iron & Steel Institute (AISI). It was created by the U.S. Steel Company, and turned over to the AISI to promote the steel industry as a whole.

The logo contains three diamond shapes, known as hypocycloids, and their three colors represent three materials used to produce steel—yellow for coal, orange for ore, and blue for steel scrap.

Republic Steel suggested the Steelers use the Steelmark as the team's logo.

The Steelers had to get permission from the AISI to change the word "Steel" inside the logo to "Steelers." Permission was granted, and the Steelers had their logo.

4. Did you know that football players didn't wear helmets during the first 27 years of football?

The first helmet was designed and worn by a player at Lafayette College, George Barclay, in 1896—but some players continued to play without helmets into the 1930s in both college ball and the NFL.

It wasn't until the late 1930s that rules were passed requiring all players to wear helmets.

5. The first NFL team to have an insignia or logo on their helmets was the Los Angeles Rams—and it was one of their players who came up with the idea.

Halfback Fred Gehrke of the 1947 Rams painted ram horns on the team's helmets, and that started the trend.

6. Amazingly, a college football team once changed the numbers on their players' uniforms EVERY week.

It happened at the University of Pittsburgh in 1915. That idea was prompted by the man who was in charge of program sales—and he changed the players' numbers every week so fans would have to buy a new program for each game.

7. Bill Cowher and Chuck Noll are in the Top Ten of all-time NFL coaches who have been head coach of the same team for the most seasons.

George Halas holds the record. He coached the Chicago Bears for 40 years.

The rest of the Top Ten are Curly Lambeau, who coached Green Bay for 29 years; Tom Landry at Dallas (29 years); Don Shula, Miami (26); Steve Owen, Giants (24); Chuck Noll, Steelers (23); Bud Grant, Minnesota (18); Hank Stram, Kansas City (15); Bill Cowher, Steelers (14); and Joe Gibbs, Washington (14).

Cowher and Gibbs are the only active coaches. Both are entering their 14th year with the same team in 2005.

8. A woman once coached a major-college football team.

When Yale was a national football power in 1892, their famous coach, Walter Camp, became ill during that season and was unable to attend practices or games. His wife, Alice, went to the practices and games for him, and served as the Yale coach that year.

Yale went undefeated.

9. A football player once scored all the points FOR BOTH TEAMS in a game.

Byron Haines of the University of Washington, in a game against Southern Cal, scored a touchdown for his team and later in the game was tackled behind his goal line, giving a safety to his opponents.

The final score was 6-2, so Haines scored all the points.

10. No Super Bowl? The NFL was in business 46 years before the first Super Bowl game was played.

The NFL started in 1920—but the first Super Bowl wasn't played until the end of the 1966 season.

11. An eight-year-old girl named the Super Bowl.

When football owners were deciding what to call their championship game, Sharron Hunt, eight-year-old daughter of Lamar Hunt, who owns the Kansas City Chiefs, had been playing with a black rubber ball called a super ball. From that she got the idea to suggest to her dad that Pro Football name its title game the Super Bowl.

Lamar Hunt made that recommendation, and so the famous Super Bowl owes its name to a little girl.

12. Former Pitt coach Johnny Majors, who led the Panthers to the national championship in 1976, had a mother and father whose names were Shirley and John—his father's name was Shirley and his mother's name was John.

His father, Shirley Majors, was a successful small-college coach. His mother was named John because that name was in the family tradition and when no boys came along in her generation she inherited the name.

13. The record for the biggest crowd ever to attend a football game was NOT set at a pro or college game as you would expect, but at a high school game.

The all-time football attendance record was at Soldier Field, Chicago, on Nov. 27, 1939, when 125,000 people came to see a high school playoff game, featuring the fabled Billy DeCorrovont.

14. How could BOTH teams lose the same football game?

This strange event happened when two Georgia high school teams played each other in 1977.

After the game, it was discovered that both teams used ineligible players. The Georgia High School Association then gave both teams a loss on their records.

15. One of football's most famous songs, the Notre Dame "Victory March" that starts out "Cheer, cheer for old Notre Dame" was written, of all places, on a church organ.

One day after a football game in 1909, Father Michael Shea decided that Notre Dame should have a good fight song, and he would write it. So Father Shea went to a nearby building that had a piano, but someone was using the piano.

Father Shea then went to the Sacred Heart Church on campus and composed the song on the organ at the church. His brother John then added the words, and Notre Dame had its great song.

16. You probably won't believe this one, but it's true. There was once a major-college football game that had a paid attendance of one.

It was the Washington State-San Jose game of Nov. 12, 1955, played at Washington State. The temperature that day was 14 below zero, and only one person showed up to pay his way into the stadium.

This unbelievable fact has been verified by the Washington State Athletic Department.

17. The smallest school ever to play in the Rose Bowl game was a little college in western Pennsylvania.

Did you know that Washington & Jefferson College of Washington, Pa. played in the Rose Bowl game of 1922?

W&J, which had just about 400 students then, tied the mighty University of California team in that Rose Bowl, 0-0.

18. Surprisingly, at one time in the NFL, ball carriers could get up and keep running AFTER they were tackled.

Plays ended only when runners were held down. That rule wasn't changed until 1955.

19. What has been called the most famous newspaper story in sports? It was Grantland Rice's report when he covered the Notre Dame-Army game on Oct. 18, 1924, and coined the nickname for football's great backfield, the Four Horsemen.

Rice wrote, "Outlined against a blue-gray October sky, the Four Horsemen rode again. In dramatic lore, they are known as famine, pestilence, destruction and death. These are only aliases. Their real names are Stuhldreher, Miller, Crowley, and Layden. They formed the crest of the South Bend cyclone ... as Notre Dame beat Army."

The Four Horsemen played together for three years, winning 27 games and losing to only one team—Nebraska.

20. Can you imagine a football coach not losing any game for 11 consecutive seasons?

The legendary Gil Dobie NEVER lost a game during his first 11 years as a coach.

His amazing streak started at North Dakota State in 1906 and 1907, where he had two undefeated teams, and continued at the University of Washington from 1908 through 1916, where his record was 58-0 with three ties.

After 11 years of coaching, Dobie finally found out what it was like to lose when he lost a game in 1917— 12 years after he started.

DID YOU KNOW...

21. One of the most unbelievable football series of all time was between Pitt and Fordham.

They played three games in 1935, '36 and '37 and, amazingly, NEITHER team scored ANY points in ANY OF THOSE GAMES.

They played three straight 0-0 games.

22. An NFL team goes to the dogs.

There was an NFL team in 1922 and 1923 that went by the name of "Oorang"—and if you look at the standings for those years, you'll see Oorang won two games in 1922 and one game in 1923.

Oorang played out of Marion, Ohio, and was named after the Oorang Dog Kennels of Marion, which owned the team.

23. It's hard to believe now, but there were 30,000 empty seats at the first Super Bowl.

That first Super Bowl was played between the Green Bay Packers and Kansas City Chiefs at the 93,000-seat Los Angeles Coliseum.

The attendance was 63,000.

24. A football once exploded during a game—and caused a team to lose.

It happened in the 1929 Rose Bowl. Benny Lom of California punted from his own 9-yard line, but his kick punctured the ball. All the air came out, and the ball collapsed right on the 9. Georgia Tech took over and scored the winning touchdown.

★ ★ ★ ★ ★

25. Incredibly, an NFL team failed to score any points in their first four games one season—and yet they won the championship of the league that season.

The Chicago Bears opened the 1932 season playing three straight 0-0 games. Then they lost their fourth game, 2-0.

Thus, in those first four games they had never crossed the goal line, kicked a field goal, or scored in any way.

But they wound up in first place with the odd record of seven wins, one loss and six ties. That turned out to be the best record in the NFL that year.

26. Surprisingly, at one time, the passer on most football teams was NOT the quarterback.

Before the T-formation became popular starting in the 1940s, passing almost always was done by a halfback. In fact, quarterbacks seldom handled the ball.

In the single and double wing formations used by most teams before the T-formation, quarterbacks were used only as blockers.

27. A man once played in an NFL game even though he had never seen a game in his life until he took the field that day.

Garo Yepremian, a soccer player from Cyprus, was visiting the U.S. when he was urged to try out with the Detroit Lions during the season.

He was hired on the spot and kicked off that week in the Lions game against the Baltimore Colts on Oct. 16, 1966—playing in the first American football game he ever saw.

28. One of the strangest football games ever played happened in the NFL in a 1988 playoff game between the Bears and Eagles.

Although more than 65,000 people were at the game, and millions more watched on TV, most fans at the game and viewers at home did NOT see many of the plays in that game.

Heavy fog had rolled into Chicago's Soldier Field. It blocked the visibility of fans in the stands and of the TV cameras.

That playoff game went down in history as the "Fog Bowl."

★ ★ ★ ★ ★

29. There was once a football game when a PLAYER—and not a pass—was thrown for a touchdown.

Tennessee lined up for a play on the Alabama 1-yard line. Running back Sam McAllester got the ball, and several of his teammates then picked him up and threw him across the goal line for a touchdown.

That happened in the early years of football and soon after that, rules were changed to prohibit that play. But throwing a player for a TD enabled Tennessee to win that game 7-0.

30. Amazingly, they once almost ran out of footballs at an NFL championship game.

When the Bears beat the Redskins 73-0 in the 1940 title game, there were 10 useable footballs on hand, which was the custom then.

When the score got to 66-0, the teams were using the only ball left because the others had been kicked into the stands on extra points. There were no nets to keep footballs from going into the stands then.

Officials asked the Bears NOT to kick an extra point after their last touchdown so they could save the only football left.

★ ★ ★ ★ ★

31. Long before today's Bowl Championship Series, there was a post-season football bowl game in which the federal government picked the two teams to play.

It happened in 1930 when the government ordered Army and Navy to meet in a game called the Charity Bowl in New York to raise money for the unemployed.

Army won, 6-0, in the only bowl game ever staged by the government.

32. The most amazing rushing record ever seen in high school, college, or Pro Football was set by Ken Hall of Sugar Land High in Texas in a game in 1953.

Hall gained 520 yards on 11 carries—meaning he AVERAGED 47 yards EACH time he carried the ball.

33. One of the zaniest games in football history was the 1950 Ohio State-Michigan game.

A blizzard covered the field with snow, obliterating all yard markers. Conditions were so bad that almost 30,000 ticketholders were unable to get to the stadium. Those who did come had trouble seeing through the swirling snow.

It was almost impossible to run or pass. In fact, Michigan NEVER completed a pass and NEVER even made a first down in the game—yet Michigan won 9-3. They scored their nine points by getting a touchdown and a safety on two blocked punts.

34. The first woman to play in a Division I-A football game was Katie Hnida.

She attempted an extra point following a New Mexico touchdown in the Las Vegas Bowl in 2002.

Unfortunately, Hnida had her kick blocked in the 27-13 loss to UCLA.

But Hnida did become the first woman to score in a Division I-A game when she kicked two extra points for New Mexico in a 72-8 win against Texas State-San Marcos in September 2003.

★ ★ ★ ★ ★

35. In a bizarre football moment, the great all-time All-American back, Tom Harmon of Michigan, not only had to run through the entire University of California team to score on an 86-yard touchdown gallop in a 1940 game at Cal—but he also had to fight off a fan from the stands.

As Harmon was running down the field to cap a big day, Bud Brennan, a spectator at Memorial Stadium, was getting tired of seeing Harmon gain so much ground all day against his beloved Cal team.

So Brennan jumped out of his seat, went on the field at the 3-yard line, and tried to stop Harmon. But it didn't bother Harmon.

He stiff-armed Brennan, pushed him out of his way, and continued to the goal line for another TD in a Michigan 41-0 rout of Cal.

36. Incredibly, there was once an NFL game when one team was behind 21-0 BEFORE THEY HAD THEIR FIRST PLAY FROM SCRIMMAGE.

It happened in 1975. San Diego kicked off to Cincinnati, and Cincinnati marched down the field for a touchdown. San Diego then fumbled the next two kickoffs and both were turned into TDs by Cincinnati.

The score was 21-0 before San Diego finally ran their first scrimmage play. (Final score was Cincinnati 47, San Diego 17).

DID YOU KNOW...

37. Talk about defense.

The Waco Texas High School team of 1921 had such a great defense that they not only didn't allow any team to score against them all season—but they also didn't allow any team to get past their 35-yard line in any game that year.

38. Did you know there was once a football game called the "Confusion Bowl" by sports writers and broadcasters? It happened when Miami played Miami.

That was a game between the only two schools in major-college football who have the same school name—Miami of Florida and Miami of Ohio.

They played against each other in 1945, and then played again in 1946.

39. Surprisingly, most of the greatest quarterbacks in NFL history NEVER won the Heisman Trophy in college football—including Terry Bradshaw, Joe Montana, Steve Young, Brett Favre, Dan Marino, Sammy Baugh, Johnny Unitas, Troy Aikman, John Elway, Payton Manning and Tom Brady.

40. Did you ever stop to think that one of the strangest words we use in football is "touchdown"?

There is NO rule in football requiring a player to touch the ball to the ground when he scores a "touchdown."

41. The most unusual road trip ever taken by a football team was the one by Willamette University of Salem, Oregon.

Willamette traveled to Hawaii for a game against the University of Hawaii on Dec. 6, 1941. But the Japanese bombing of Pearl Harbor occurred the next morning—and the team was stranded on the island.

Many team members were finally able to return to Oregon in early 1942, serving as aides on a hospital ship. But some of the players didn't conclude the road trip UNTIL 1945, since they immediately enlisted in the military and were shipped to the South Pacific to fight in World War II.

42. Here's the story of a football team that won by losing.

Boston College was the No. 1 team in the country in 1942. They were undefeated going into their last game against Holy Cross.

BC was heavily favored and made reservations to hold a victory celebration after the game at a place called the Cocoanut Grove.

However, in one of the greatest upsets in college football history, Holy Cross not only beat BC, but they beat them by the score of 55-12. The crushed Boston College officials cancelled the "victory" party.

That night, the Cocoanut Grove caught fire. It was one of the worst disasters in U.S. history with 492 people losing their lives. The Boston College football players all might have been killed—except for the fact that they lost a football game that afternoon.

43. Several teams have won the Super Bowl two years in a row—but no team has ever won it more than two consecutive years.

The teams that have won two straight Super Bowls are: Green Bay 1967-68, Miami 1973-74, Pittsburgh 1975-76,

Pittsburgh 1979-80, San Francisco 1989-90, Dallas 1993-94, Denver 1998-99, and New England 2004-05.

Likewise, surprisingly, no major-college team has won the national championship more than two years in a row in all the years since the Associated Press started its annual polls in 1936.

44. Believe it or not, the NFL championship game one year was played on a field that was only 80 yards long.

The title game of 1932 was scheduled for Chicago, but a blizzard came along and officials moved the game indoors to an arena where the longest they could make the field was 80 yards.

Despite such a short field, there was hardly any scoring.

The Chicago Bears won 9-0, scoring just one touchdown and one safety.

45. Amazingly, there was once a football team that after playing its first five games one season still had neither a win NOR a loss.

Wofford College of South Carolina opened the 1948 season by playing five straight tie games. That's the all-time record in college football.

46. A player once GAVE AWAY the Heisman Trophy he won—but it was one of the most emotional events in college football history.

John Cappelletti of Penn State won the Heisman in 1973. At the awards ceremony that year, Cappelletti said he never would have won the trophy without the motivation from his 11-year-old brother, Joey, who was fighting leukemia.

During his acceptance speech, without a dry eye in the room, John said, "They say I showed courage on the football field, but Joey lives in pain all the time. His courage is round the clock. I want him to have the trophy. It's more his than mine because he's been such an inspiration."

With that, John gave the Heisman Trophy to Joey, who kept it by his bed until he died two years later.

47. What are the odds that two boys from the same small-town high school would both wind up in the Pro Football Hall of Fame?

The great passer Sammy Baugh and the great center Bulldog Turner both made the select company of the Pro Football Hall of Fame—and both came from Sweetwater Texas High School.

48. There was once a great football team that never existed.

In 1941, a group of Wall Street stockbrokers got together and invented a college football team that they named Plainfield State Teachers College.

They began calling newspapers each week, giving the score of Plainfield's imaginary games. Newspapers, assuming the scores were real, printed them each Sunday. As the season went on, the stockbrokers had Plainfield undefeated, untied and unscored on, and they sent out feature stories about the team.

Finally, the hoax was revealed and Plainfield went down in history as the great team that never was.

DID YOU KNOW...

49. In the history of big-time football, no player ever had a day like Red Grange of Illinois had against Michigan on Oct. 18, 1924.

The first time Grange got the ball, he ran 95 yards for a touchdown. The second time he got the ball, he ran 67 yards for a TD. The third time he got the ball, he ran 56 yards for a TD. And the fourth time he got the ball, he ran 44 yards for a TD.

He had taken the ball four times, scored four times, covered 262 yards, and still had not been stopped or tackled.

50. One of the most amazing football players of all time was Ellis Jones.

Not only did Jones play major-college football with one arm, but he won All-America honors and played first string on teams that went to three straight bowl games.

Jones, who had lost his right arm in a childhood accident, was a starting guard for the University of Tulsa in 1942-43-44. With Jones as a starter, Tulsa won 23 games, lost only two and tied one, and played in the Sugar Bowl twice and the Orange Bowl once.

51. It's hard to believe a player on the LOSING team in the Super Bowl would be voted the Most Valuable Player for that game—but that's what happened in 1971.

The MVP of Super Bowl V in 1971 was linebacker Chuck Howley of Dallas, even though Dallas lost that game, 16-13, to Baltimore.

52. Incredibly, a major-college football coach once insisted that officials TAKE AWAY a touchdown his team had scored.

It happened when this coach noticed a penalty on the play that the officials had missed.

The coach was the legendary Amos Alonzo Stagg, who was so strict that he wouldn't accept a touchdown his team had scored when he knew they had committed a penalty on that play.

53. One of the most famous games in NFL history was the "Heidi Game"—and here's how it got that name.

The New York Jets were playing the Oakland Raiders in 1968. NBC was televising the game nationally, and ended the telecast with two minutes remaining so they could air, on time, at 7 p.m. Eastern time, the children's classic movie, "Heidi."

The Jets were leading 32-29, but then the Raiders scored two touchdowns in those last two minutes and came from behind to win 43-32.

TV viewers never saw that rally. There was a huge public outcry—and the game went into football lore as the "Heidi Game."

★ ★ ★ ★ ★

54. Ever hear of the "invisible field goal"?

This strange field goal was kicked by Pat Summerall of the New York Giants against the Cleveland Browns, and decided a key game in 1958.

Summerall, the Giants kicker who later went on to a career as a TV announcer, booted the ball in the closing seconds of a 10-10 tie into a swirling snowstorm.

The ball went up in the air and was completely lost from view in the snow. Nobody could see the ball.

Then all of a sudden, the ball reappeared, dropped down over the goal post, and gave the Giants the win and a playoff berth—with that "invisible" field goal.

55. A college football player once ran 210 yards for one touchdown.

Playing for Lehigh College in 1918, Snooks Dowd picked off a fumble near his opponent's goal line—but then ran the wrong way, going down the length of the field, 100 yards. He realized his error, made a U-turn around his own end zone, and started up the field, running 110 yards back to the right goal line.

He scored what has been called the only 210-yard TD in history.

56. The Pittsburgh Steelers and Philadelphia Eagles could not join the NFL during the league's early years for a very good reason.

The NFL requires its teams to play most of its games on Sundays—but the State of Pennsylvania had a law prohibiting Sunday games (and movies, too) until 1933.

Only when the law was repealed in a close vote were the Steelers and Eagles able to join the NFL.

★ ★ ★ ★ ★

57. The H.J. Heinz Company is the only multinational company in the world headed by the son of a former National Football League head coach.

Heinz's chairman, president and CEO is William R. Johnson.

Johnson is the son of Bill "Tiger" Johnson, who was head coach of the Cincinnati Bengals in the NFL from 1976 to 1978.

CHAPTER 3

FUN FACTS ABOUT FOOTBALL STADIUMS

STADIUM FUN FACTS

Did you know that the shape and size of one particular stadium changed the game of football—and gave us football as we know it today.

This story begins with the building of Harvard Stadium in 1903.

That stadium was the world's first massive, reinforced-concrete structure and the first large, permanent arena for American football.

But at that time, football was so rough that there were debates around the country about outlawing it altogether. Players were dying every year as the result of football injuries, and that caused President Theodore Roosevelt to step in.

Roosevelt called a meeting of coaches and athletic directors in 1904 to see what could be done about lessening the dangers of the game. At that meeting, one suggestion was to widen the field by 40 feet to give players more room to run, and alleviate the close-in line play that was causing so many injuries.

In a historic moment, the coach at Harvard raised his hand and told President Roosevelt and the assembled group that Harvard had just built its magnificent new stadium and, with the close proximity of the concrete stands to the field, there was no way Harvard could widen the field of play.

STADIUM FUN FACTS

In fact, he said, the field could not be wider than 53-and-one-third yards (the width of today's gridirons).

Because of Harvard's prestige and its place as a football power at that time, the group agreed they'd have to come up with another solution to make the game safer.

A little background about the origin and development of football is necessary here to understand the situation of the game at the time of President Roosevelt's meeting.

The first American football game was played in 1869, and passing wasn't allowed at all. In fact, the game evolved from British soccer and was much like soccer, where only goaltenders were allowed to touch the ball with their hands. Then, gradually, the American rules were changed to permit running with the ball. Finally, in the late 1800s, the forward pass was legalized in limited situations, but few teams took advantage of it. Instead, they slugged it out at the line of scrimmage, resulting in the alarming number of injuries and even deaths. Many teams went through entire games without passing at all.

The solution to the problem that the President's group finally proposed was a revolutionary change. They legislated more forward passing and other rules changes to open up the game and lessen injuries —without having to widen the field.

Thus, they made the game safer and more appealing, while saving a famous stadium.

So, because of a stadium—Harvard Stadium—football was changed forever. The forward pass increasingly became part of the game, and eventually gave us football as we know it now.

The original Harvard Stadium, by the way, is still in use and is the oldest football stadium in America today. It also has an NFL connection. The Boston (now New England) Patriots played their first game there in their first season, in 1960.

The next great milestone in football stadiums after Harvard Stadium was built in 1903 came when Yale opened its historic Yale Bowl in 1914. It is now the second-oldest active stadium in the country—and was the first bowl-shaped stadium ever built for football.

STADIUM FUN FACTS

Interestingly, when the NFL began in the 1920s, its teams generally played not in their own stadiums or even in existing college football stadiums—but in major league baseball parks. Among the reasons were that pro teams, new at the time, did not have the finances to build their own stadiums and, because they were considered a threat, they were generally not welcome on college campuses.

Early NFL teams such as the Chicago Bears played their games at the baseball Cubs' Wrigley Field; the New York Giants played at their baseball namesake's Polo Grounds; the Washington Redskins played at the old Washington baseball park, Griffith Stadium; and the Pittsburgh Steelers played at the baseball Pirates' Forbes Field.

The original Green Bay Packers went one step further. They played at an old field owned by the local Hagermeister Brewery, with just a small supply of bleachers and no built-in clubhouses. Players dressed elsewhere and, at half-time, just relaxed at one end of the field with fans gathered around them, listening to the coach speak.

STADIUM FUN FACTS

The oldest NFL stadium being used today is Soldier Field in Chicago. Although the stadium first opened in 1924, the Bears didn't move there until 1971. Other current NFL stadiums built before 1990 are those in Arizona, Buffalo, Dallas, Green Bay, Indianapolis, Kansas City, the Meadowlands, Miami, Minnesota, New Orleans, Oakland, San Diego, and San Francisco. Pittsburgh's Heinz Field opened in 2001.

The NFL franchises that have played home games in the most stadiums are the St. Louis Rams, New England Patriots, Tennessee Titans and Philadelphia Eagles. The Rams have had seven different home stadiums, while the Patriots, Titans and Eagles have each called six different fields home.

The Rams began their existence in Cleveland, where they played at the old baseball field, League Park; then moved to Shaw Stadium and Municipal Stadium before departing Cleveland for Los Angeles. In the L.A. area, the Rams played at the Coliseum and at Anaheim Stadium. Then they moved to St. Louis' Busch Stadium and, eventually, their seventh home, the Edward Jones Dome.

STADIUM FUN FACTS

The Patriots have played at Harvard Stadium, Boston University's Nickerson Field, Boston College's Alumni Stadium, the Red Sox's Fenway Park, Foxboro Stadium, and the current Gillette Stadium.

The Titans, who started in Houston, have used the following as home fields: Jeppeesen Stadium, Rice Stadium and the Astrodome in Houston; the Liberty Bowl in Memphis; and Vanderbilt Stadium and the Coliseum in Nashville.

The Eagles' six home fields have been the Phillies' old ballpark, Baker Bowl; the A's former home, Shibe Park; Municipal Stadium; the University of Pennsylvania's Franklin Field; Veterans Stadium; and the new Lincoln Financial Field.

There are four football stadiums in America that seat more than 100,000 spectators.

The biggest is the University of Michigan's with more than 107,000 seats.

Others with 100,000-plus capacity are Beaver Stadium at Penn State, Neyland Stadium at the University of Tennessee, and Ohio Stadium at Ohio State.

STADIUM FUN FACTS

The largest stadium not located on a college campus is the Rose Bowl in Pasadena, California, which seats 98,636.

Two NFL teams NEVER play a home game in their home state. The New York Giants and New York Jets both play home games at Giants Stadium in East Rutherford, New Jersey.

And, the Washington Redskins' stadium is not in Washington, D.C., but in Raljon, Maryland.

One of history's biggest scientific discoveries was made—of all places—at a football field.

On Dec. 2, 1942, scientists working under the stands at the University of Chicago's football stadium created the first controlled nuclear chain reaction—and, at that instant, the Atomic Age was born.

Chicago had given up football three years earlier, making their stadium available for the top-secret atomic experiments.

STADIUM FUN FACTS

Ever wonder why post-season football games are called "bowl games"?

That phrase came into our language because of a stadium—a new stadium.

In 1923, Pasadena's originally-named Tournament of Roses game moved into a newly-built, bowl-shaped stadium.

A local publicity man named both the stadium and the game the "Rose Bowl." After that, other post-season games called themselves "bowl games" even though many of them are NOT played in circular, bowl-like stadiums.

The Pittsburgh Steelers spent the first 31 years of their existence playing their home games at the Pirates' ballpark, Forbes Field.

The Steelers played at Forbes Field from 1933 until 1964, when they moved to Pitt Stadium. They stayed at Pitt Stadium through 1969 before moving to Three Rivers Stadium in 1970.

STADIUM FUN FACTS

After 31 years of sharing Three Rivers with baseball's Pittsburgh Pirates, the Steelers moved into their beautiful new Heinz Field in 2001—and brought their former landlords, the Pitt Panthers, with them.

CHAPTER 4

HEINZ FIELD
HIGHLIGHTS

Largest scoreboard in the nation?

Did you know that when the scoreboard at Heinz Field was installed in 2001, it was indeed the largest anywhere in the United States.

The Heinz Field scoreboard has a gigantic display area that's 96 feet wide by 27 feet high.

In keeping with the team's name, the Steelers' home stadium, Heinz Field, was built with lots of steel—more than 12,000 tons of structural steel.

How much did Heinz pay for the naming rights to Heinz Field? The amount has a 57 in it, natch! The amount is $57 million.

ON THE FIELD

Heinz is investing an average of $2.85 million a year for 20 years for the $57 million naming rights fee—and that yearly amount is closely equivalent to airing just one 30-second commercial during the Super Bowl.

One reason the name "Heinz Field" was selected instead of Heinz Stadium is that the turf is natural grass—which was not the case at Three Rivers Stadium.

According to all available research, Steelers wide receiver Hines Ward is the only player in NFL history whose home stadium is pronounced the same as his first name.

A unique feature of Heinz Field—seen in no other football stadium—are the two giant ketchup bottles that come to life when the Steelers or Pitt Panthers enter the red zone.

ON THE FIELD

Excitement builds as the two Heinz Ketchup bottles tilt downward, their bottle caps flip up, and red light-emitting diodes flow downward, simulating ketchup pouring out of the bottles. The pouring action triggers animation on the scoreboard, encouraging fan participation.

The two gigantic Heinz Ketchup bottles on the Heinz Field scoreboard are each 35 feet long, 9 feet high, 6 feet deep, and weigh 8,000 pounds.

They made their debut during a Monday night game on Oct. 29, 2001, when the Steelers entered the red zone and went on to defeat the Tennessee Titans.

If both of the scoreboard bottles were emptied, the virtual equivalent of 1,664,000 fluid ounces of Heinz Ketchup would pour out...enough to add zest to approximately 3.2 million hotdogs, or coat the field with 3/4-inches of ketchup!

The two scoreboard ketchup bottles at Heinz Field are the two largest Heinz Ketchup bottles in the world.

After 68 years in the NFL, the Steelers finally got a home stadium built to their own specifications with the opening of Heinz Field in 2001. Previously, the Steelers' homes were the Pirates' Forbes Field, Pitt's Pitt Stadium and the baseball-football stadium, Three Rivers.

When Steelers chairman Dan Rooney broke ground for Heinz Field in 1999, he used the same shovel with which his dad, Art Rooney, Sr., broke ground for Three Rivers Stadium 30 years earlier.

That statue outside Gate 1 of Heinz Field is a larger-than-life likeness of "The Chief," Art Rooney, Sr. (with his ever-present cigar), who founded the Steelers in 1933.

One reason Heinz Field is horseshoe-shaped is to provide an open end that offers fans in the stands and TV viewers a vista of Pittsburgh's downtown skyline.

ON THE FIELD

A must-see destination for fans at Heinz Field is the Coca-Cola® Great Hall under the east side stands. The Hall features fascinating football memorabilia from the Pitt Panthers and the Pittsburgh Steelers.

When the Pitt Panthers moved into Heinz Field in 2001, they ended many years of playing their home football games at Pitt Stadium. The Panthers had called Pitt Stadium their home for the previous 76 seasons.

Just like the Steelers, Pitt at one time played its home football games at the Pirates' Forbes Field. Pitt played at Forbes Field in the years before the opening of Pitt Stadium in 1925.

ON THE FIELD

The Heinz Field ground crew is kept exceptionally busy when Pitt plays a home game on Saturday and the Steelers play the next day. The crew has less than 24 hours to change the field's hash marks from the college to pro requirements, and to change the end zone and field logos.

Although Heinz Field is one of the most beautiful football venues in America, oddly enough, the first event ever held there was NOT a football game. Heinz Field was inaugurated with a concert by 'N SYNC in August 2001.

One of the biggest thrills experienced by high school football players is to play a game at a big-league stadium such as Heinz Field, where All-Pros and All-Americans trod. Heinz Field has been the site of high school playoff games every year since its first season in 2001.

ON THE FIELD

Pittsburgh was selected as the site of the 2005 Bassmaster Classic, in part, because of the vibrant urban backdrop for the world's top bass anglers and their fans. Part of that background for those in attendance and for television viewers was Heinz Field, as anglers fished for bass in the Allegheny River in front of the stadium.

Bassmaster, the world championship of bass fishing, was first held in 1971 on Nevada's Lake Mead. Anglers qualify for the Classic through several rigorous tournaments.

When watching a game played at *Heinz* Field, football fans naturally *relish* victories by their team. When their team gets behind in a game, they root for them to play *ketchup* football and pour it on!

- They like to see their quarterback put some *mustard* on the ball and be a *smart one*.

- Nothing better than to have the other team in a *pickle*.

CHAPTER 5

1869—WHEN HEINZ AND FOOTBALL WERE BORN

... AND OTHER FUN FACTS ABOUT HEINZ

★ ★ ★ ★ ★

ALL ABOUT HEINZ

The "H.J." in the H.J. Heinz Company name comes from the initials of the company founder's first and middle names. He was Henry John Heinz.

Henry John Heinz was born in Pittsburgh in 1844.

By the time he was 12, Henry was selling produce from his mother Anna's backyard vegetable garden to neighbors, door-to-door.

The year the first football game was played in America, 1869, was the same year Henry Heinz first formed his company to process and market food products.

That first football game played in America was a college game on the campus of Rutgers University in New Brunswick, N.J., on Nov. 6, 1869. Rutgers met and defeated Princeton, 6-4.

Henry Heinz's first manufactured product in 1869 was not ketchup as many would guess, but bottled horseradish, made from his mother's own special recipe.

ALL ABOUT HEINZ

After introducing horseradish to get his Heinz company started, Henry next turned to celery sauce, mustard, sauerkraut and pickles.

One of the world's best-known products—Heinz® Ketchup—was born in 1876. Today, Heinz produces more than 1.4 BILLION bottles of ketchup every year.

In addition to the 1.4 billion bottles of ketchup, Heinz makes more than 11 billion packets of ketchup and dressings each year—that's at least two packets for every person on earth.

You can find Heinz Ketchup almost anywhere you go, in 140 countries around the world.

Ketchup was invented by the Chinese, and the word "ketchup" comes from variations of the Asian words "ketsiap" and "kechap."

In June 2004, Heinz Ketchup "came home" to the place where ketchup was born—China.

ALL ABOUT HEINZ

Already a favorite in China, Heinz Ketchup will have a big presence at the 2008 Summer Olympic Games in Beijing. The Beijing Olympic Training Center includes a Heinz Restaurant that features, naturally, Heinz Ketchup and other Heinz goodies.

Today Heinz is recognized as the most global of all U.S.-based food companies.

Heinz products are sold on all of the six inhabited continents of the world—Africa, Asia, Europe, North America, Oceania (including Australia) and South America.

Although there are no supermarkets on the seventh continent in the world, Antarctica, Heinz products have been seen in kitchens and dining rooms there.

Heinz's brands hold No. 1 or No. 2 market positions in more than 50 countries.

ALL ABOUT HEINZ

Until ketchup became Heinz's best-selling product in the 1880s, Heinz's No. 1 seller was pickles.

The longest-running advertising giveaway by any company is the Heinz pickle pin, first offered at the Chicago World's Fair in 1893.

In the years since 1893, Heinz has given away more than 50 million pickle pins, and many are saved as a popular collectible.

You still can get a Heinz pickle pin by writing to:

> Heinz Pickle Pin
> P.O. Box 57
> Pittsburgh, PA 15230

Heinz introduced a ketchup pin to go with the pickle pin on New Year's Day 2000. On that day, Heinz gave away 57,000 ketchup pins around the world.

To get your ketchup pin, write to:

> Heinz Ketchup Pin
> P.O. Box 57
> Pittsburgh, PA 15230

ALL ABOUT HEINZ

Heinz products around the world (besides the Heinz brand) include such brand names as Ore-Ida®, SmartOnes®, Bagel Bites®, Plasmon®, Wattie's®, San Marco®, Farley's®, John West, Petit Navire, Greenseas®, Classico®, Wyler's®, UFC®, Orlando®, ABC®, Honig®, De Ruijter, Olivine and Pudliszki.

Heinz also uses the famous names of Weight Watchers, Boston Market, T.G.I. Friday's, Jack Daniel's, and Linda McCartney under license.

The original Heinz plant and offices were just a little way up the Allegheny River from today's Heinz Field.

Now, more than 130 years after Heinz's beginning, its world headquarters are in downtown Pittsburgh, a mile or so from Heinz Field.

Heinz products sit atop 100 million restaurant tables every day.

Did you know that Heinz is one of the very few companies in the world to lead in market share in so many different products in so many different countries? Just three examples:

- Heinz Ketchup has a 60% retail share in the U.S.
- Heinz baby food in Australia has a 74% share.
- Heinz beans in the UK have a 67% share.

It turns out that ketchup is not only good, but it's also good for you. That's because ketchup is made from lycopene-rich tomatoes. Tests have shown that lycopene is a powerful antioxidant that may aid in reducing the risk of certain cancers and heart disease.

Lycopene is present in all tomatoes—but the human body gets even more lycopene benefits from cooked tomatoes than from uncooked ones. That's because the heating of tomatoes releases up to five times more lycopene. And, of course, Heinz Ketchup is made from tomatoes processed into paste.

ALL ABOUT HEINZ

What exactly is in ketchup? The exact recipe of Heinz Ketchup is a closely guarded secret—but the ingredients are no secret. Ingredients, besides tomatoes, include vinegar, sugar or corn syrup, salt, onions, garlic and a variety of natural spices.

The biggest advertisement in the world—in existence for 46 years—was the Heinz Pier that extended the length of almost three football fields out into the Atlantic Ocean in Atlantic City, N.J. The pier had a boardwalk, lounge, reading room, theater, sun deck, exhibit hall and organ, and displayed Heinz products with free pickle pins and food samples.

On the roof of the pier was a 70-foot-high electric sign with a huge "57" that glowed at night and could be seen for miles. The Heinz Pier was in existence from 1898 until it was destroyed by a hurricane in 1944.

The world's best-known branded potato processor is Ore-Ida®, with a U.S. share of about 50%. Heinz has owned the Ore-Ida company since 1965.

ALL ABOUT HEINZ

All the products that bear the Ore-Ida brand got their names from two neighboring states, Oregon and Idaho. The original Ore-Ida company was based in Ontario, Oregon, and Burley, Idaho, so they took the "Ore" from Oregon and the "Ida" from Idaho.

The amount of popular Ore-Ida potato products sold today is staggering. For instance, the Ore-Ida plant in Ontario, Oregon, produces enough French fries every day that, if placed end-to-end, would reach from Canada to Mexico.

Among the new Ore-Ida products that families enjoy today are the new Ore-Ida® Extra Crispy™ Fries.

Bagel Bites® (mini-pizzas) are among the most popular after-school snacks, and the company's newest brands offer the taste of Mexico with Delimex® Tacquitos.

Although Heinz reached its 136th birthday in 2005, the company has been led by just six chief executives. Meanwhile, during that same period, there have been 25 Presidents of the United States.

ALL ABOUT HEINZ

After founder Henry Heinz died in 1919, the company was run by two more family members into the 1960s: Henry's son, Howard, and then his grandson, Jack.

After almost 100 years of someone named Heinz heading the Heinz company, that string was broken when Burt Gookin was appointed CEO in 1966. Gookin was followed by Tony O'Reilly and Bill Johnson.

Johnson was named president of Heinz in 1996, and then had the titles of CEO added in 1998 and Chairman in 2000.

More than six million people see the Heinz Hitch perform every year. The Hitch, reminiscent of the wagon used for deliveries made by founder Henry Heinz himself in the early days of the company, is drawn by eight beautiful Percheron horses.

ALL ABOUT HEINZ

The Hitch has been seen on television and in person at events such as the Rose Bowl Parade, Macy's Thanksgiving Day Parade, and many other events in the U.S. and Canada.

When the Heinz Hitch appeared at the Rose Bowl Parade on New Year's Day, it was always 57th in line, honoring Heinz's "57 Varieties" slogan.

Why is it that Heinz uses the famous slogan "57 Varieties" when it really makes many more products than that? The fact is that when the slogan was first used in the early days of the company, Heinz already was selling more than 57 products. Here's the story:

Company founder Henry Heinz picked "57 Varieties" as his slogan one day when he was riding an elevated train in New York City in 1896. He looked up and saw a car-card advertising 21 varieties of shoes. He quickly decided to use that type of slogan for his company.

Henry chose "57 Varieties" for his slogan—even though his company was manufacturing more than 60 products at the time. Why did he pick 57? Henry thought it was a magic, lucky number.

He said it kept running through his mind, and the more he thought about it, the more he was convinced to use it.

When Henry told his advertising manager that he had selected "57 Varieties" for the company's new motto, the advertising man said, "But Mr. Heinz, we sell more than 57 products." Henry said, "That's all right. I'm convinced we should use that number."

Within a week, "57 Varieties" began appearing in newspapers, on billboards, signboards, and "everywhere I could find a place to stick it," according to Henry's diary.

You've heard of consecutive records in sports. It turns out that Heinz has set a consecutive record of another kind by using the same slogan for the most consecutive years—an incredible 109 straight years from 1896 through 2005. No wonder when people see "57," they think of Heinz.

And it looks as if Henry Heinz was indeed right: "57" was, and is, a lucky number for his company. Although the H.J. Heinz Company still uses "57 Varieties," they now make more than 5,700 products.

From the beginning, Henry Heinz emphasized the purity of his products by putting them in transparent jars so that shoppers could see what was inside.

ALL ABOUT HEINZ

Heinz also pioneered factory tours so the public could see the products being made.

The famous keystone-shaped label on Heinz products came about because the Heinz company was founded in Pennsylvania—the Keystone State.

The Heinz keystone trademark has become more than just an emblem or symbol. Experts say that Heinz's keystone is an icon that provides reassurance for customers and families across countries and cultures.

Customers, experts say, don't just consume an iconic brand such as Heinz; they develop a relationship with it.

Heinz is unique in that its iconic brand and keystone trademark span a number of product lines that have allowed Heinz to become one of the most trusted brands in the world.

Heinz became the largest ketchup producer in the world as long ago as 1900 and has kept that position ever since.

ALL ABOUT HEINZ

An independent marketing consulting firm recently released a report showing that the Heinz brand is one of the most valuable in the world for three basic reasons:

- First, Heinz is known for consistent quality products that stand the test of time, regardless of trends or fads.

- Second, Heinz is the most popular brand in most of the categories and countries in which it competes.

- Finally, the report shows, Heinz is always associated with great taste, good times and family values.

CHAPTER 6

THE INSIDE SCOOP
ON TAILGATING

★ ★ ★ ★ ★

THE ULTIMATE PRE-GAME PARTY

Although American football and the H.J. Heinz Company both started in 1869, it would take some 50 years after that until the popular sport of tailgating began.

The word "tailgating" with regard to football originated from the actual tailgate, or back ledge, on old station wagons that were dropped down and used as the "table" for pre-game meals.

Now, of course, real tailgaters at games often need lots more space to serve and eat their goodies.

The whole concept of football tailgating began in the 1920s in New Haven, Connecticut.

It just so happened that there were extensive lawns surrounding the Yale Bowl in New Haven, where Yale University plays its football games.

THE ULTIMATE PRE-GAME PARTY

As automobile use was increasing in the 1920s, more and more Yale grads and fans began driving to the Bowl from the New York City area to see their beloved Elis do battle.

It was those fans who started the custom of bringing food and drink with them, and serving elaborate lunches before going into the stadium to see the game.

The custom that started at New Haven gradually was copied on other college campuses, and then spread to the NFL.

Dictionaries began to recognize the word "tailgating." One dictionary described it as "a picnic that is served from the tailgate of a vehicle, as before a sports event."

To many fans, tailgating at a game or enjoying food and drink around a TV set at their own or a friend's home, is as much a part of football as the action on the field itself.

THE ULTIMATE PRE-GAME PARTY

And many would agree that tailgating is about much more than food and drink and football. It's about bringing family and friends together.

Tailgating has become a community social, and it's not just part of the pre-game experience. Tailgating has evolved into halftime, post-game and more. It's a total game-day experience.

Tailgating is a uniquely American experience. It is unheard of in Europe and elsewhere in the world.

One of the interesting features of tailgating is its variety. The original Ivy League tailgate parties at Yale were described by Jazz Age novelist F. Scott Fitzgerald as consisting of servants setting up elaborate tables covered with white linens, the finest silverware, gourmet food and champagne. Many of today's tailgaters are happy grilling hamburgers and hot dogs, and washing 'em down with a Coke® or beer.

THE ULTIMATE PRE-GAME PARTY

One NFL spokesman was quoted as saying that, for many fans, the tailgate is as big an event as the game.

How can you get the most out of your tailgate parties? We're happy to supply you with a checklist—arranged in five different categories—to help you maximize your tailgating pleasures.

You'll see that these five categories feature the things you'll want to check for your tailgating: (1) food, (2) tableware, (3) liquids, (4) grill, and—very important— (5) the miscellaneous items that can make your tailgating really special.

TAILGATING CHECKLIST

(1) Food

Main Courses
Salads
Snacks
Chips
Dressings
Ketchup
Mustard
Salt & Pepper
Barbecue Sauce
Cooler for perishable foods
Cheese
Crackers
Cookies
Desserts

(2) Tableware

Plates
Cups
Drinking glasses
Bowls
Knives, forks, spoons
Napkins
Paper towels
Toothpicks
Wet towelettes

THE ULTIMATE PRE-GAME PARTY

(3) Liquids

Water
Soft Drinks
Beer
Wine
Liquor
Lemonade
Mixes
Openers
Ice & ice packs
Cooler for beverages

(4) Grill

Grill
Charcoal
Gas tank
Spatula
Tongs
Cutting knife
Serving platters
Matches
Lighter
Pans
Cooking mitts
Brush
Latex gloves
Aluminum foil (for lining
grill and for leftovers)

THE ULTIMATE PRE-GAME PARTY

(5) Miscellaneous

TV and antenna
AC adapter
Extension cords
Radio
Folding chairs and tables
Binoculars
Rainwear and umbrellas
Awning
Camera
Blankets
Basket for carrying supplies
Basket for nonperishable foods
Football (for tossing around)
Newspapers
Sunblock
Sunglasses
Garbage bags
Car flag with team pennant

THE ULTIMATE PRE-GAME PARTY

And here are some other tips to consider for your ideal tailgating experience:

- Have sweaters, jackets, caps, etc. in team colors, proudly displaying the team's logo.

- Plan your menus well in advance, taking into account the time of year and members of your party.

- Plan your arrival and set-up times.

- Decorate your site with team colors and your unique personal identifications (balloons, etc.), so your site can be easily found by invited guests (and yourself after the game).

- Make a point to meet your tailgate neighbors.

- Be sure the food is ready on time.

- Make sure your car has a first-aid kit.

THE ULTIMATE PRE-GAME PARTY

- Use an old toolbox to hold knives, forks, spoons, and miscellaneous items.

- When leaving, clean the area (which will help make sure you left nothing behind).

- Plan for the next game!

FOOD AND FOOTBALL— A WINNING COMBINATION!

What could be better than the smell of the charcoal grill and the sizzling aroma of chops, burgers or chicken with all the fixin's wafting through the parking lot at a Steelers game—or at home—as you prepare to watch the Black & Gold on TV?

To enhance your football-watching pleasure, or to enjoy after the game's over or anytime, we've created the best darn tailgating recipes ever—all made better with one or more of the many flavorful Heinz® condiments, marinades, and other fine products.

Prepare to tantalize your taste buds with our 57 specially selected recipes created just for Heinz and Heinz Field. And there are even three bonus recipes—the famous Heinz Love Apple Pie, Tic Tac Toe cookies, and the winning recipe from the 2005 Heinz Tailgate Playoff Recipe Contest. Enjoy—and GO STEELERS!

Rania L. Harris
Certified Chef & Owner
Rania's Catering, Mt. Lebanon, Pennsylvania

CHAPTER 7

57 SPECIAL TAILGATING RECIPES AND COOKING TIPS

★ ★ ★ ★ ★

BAKED BRIE WITH CRANBERRY CHUTNEY

Ingredients:

Brie:
1 2-1/2-pound wheel of brie, rind left on
Cranberry chutney (see recipe below)
French bread, heated, sliced

Chutney:
2/3 cup sugar
1-1/3 cups cranberries
4 teaspoons Heinz® Apple Cider Vinegar
1/3 cup raisins
1/4 cup coarsely chopped walnuts
2 teaspoons light-brown sugar
1/4 teaspoon ground ginger
1/2 teaspoon chopped garlic

Directions:

Chutney: Combine 2/3 cup water and sugar in a heavy, 3-quart saucepan over medium-high heat. Stir to dissolve the sugar; then bring to a boil without stirring. Add the cranberries, vinegar, raisins, walnuts, brown sugar, ginger, and garlic. Boil very slowly, stirring occasionally, until fairly thick. Allow to cool to room temperature. Cover and refrigerate.

Place a sheet of parchment on rimless baking sheet. Place brie in center. Spread cranberry chutney over top of cheese. Refrigerate for at least 30 minutes before baking. Preheat oven to 350 degrees.

Place brie on center shelf and bake until heated through, about 8 to 10 minutes. Watch carefully. Remove from oven and serve with french bread.

Serves: 20 as an hors d'oeuvre

TIP: Be sure that brie is well-chilled before baking. Never over-bake brie, as it will melt and run.

CHILI CHEESE FRIES

Ingredients:

1 pound lean ground beef
2 tablespoons chili powder
1-1/2 tablespoons dried
    oregano
1 teaspoon ground
    cinnamon
2 14-1/2-ounce cans stewed
    tomatoes
1-1/2 tablespoons Heinz®
    Red Wine Vinegar
Ore-Ida® Zesty Fries™
Grated cheddar cheese

Directions:

Sauté the beef in a heavy, large skillet over medium-high heat 4 minutes, breaking up the meat with the back of a fork. Mix in the chili powder, oregano and cinnamon. Add the tomatoes and bring to a simmer, breaking up large tomato pieces with fork. Reduce heat, cover and simmer until chili thickens slightly, about 3 minutes. Stir often. Add vinegar; season chili to taste with salt and pepper.

Bake Ore-Ida Zesty Fries according to package directions.

Place fries on a large serving platter, and top with chili and cheddar cheese. Serve immediately.

Serves: 4

TIP: Always drain all excess fat from the beef after you've sautéed it. Then proceed with the recipe.

BARBECUED PEANUT CHICKEN WINGS

Ingredients:
12 chicken wings
1/2 pound bacon—sliced
   thin
1/4 cup dry sherry
2 tablespoons honey
2 tablespoons Heinz® 57
   Sauce
Freshly ground black pepper
   to taste
2/3 cup chopped raw
   peanuts
1/2 cup soy sauce
2 tablespoons brown
   sugar—packed
2 tablespoons hoisin sauce
1 clove garlic—minced

Directions:
Remove wing tips and
cut wings into 2 pieces
at the joint.

Combine soy sauce, sherry,
brown sugar, honey, hoisin
sauce, Heinz 57 Sauce,
garlic, and pepper. Add
wings, chill and marinate 6
hours or overnight.

Add bacon and marinate
5 minutes.

Coat wings with peanuts
and wrap with bacon.

Arrange wings on a rack in
a foil-lined roasting pan.

Bake in a preheated oven
20–30 minutes at 375
degrees, until golden brown
and crispy. Serve hot.

Serves: 4 as an appetizer

TIP: Store wing tips in a
zipped bag in your freezer
and save them for your next
batch of homemade chicken
stock.

CAROLINA SPICY SHRIMP

Ingredients:

3 cups water seasoned with
   Old Bay® Seasoning
1/2 cup vegetable oil
1/4 cup Heinz® Ketchup
1/4 cup Heinz® Apple Cider
   Vinegar
1/2 tablespoon Heinz®
   Worcestershire Sauce
1-1/2 teaspoons light-brown
   sugar
1/4 teaspoon salt
1/4 teaspoon dry mustard
TABASCO® sauce to taste
3 bay leaves (fresh if
   possible)
2 pounds shrimp—peeled
   and deveined (15–18
   count)
1 cup onion slices

Directions:

Bring the water seasoned
with the Old Bay Seasoning
to a boil.

In a bowl, combine the
vegetable oil, ketchup,
vinegar, worcestershire
sauce, sugar, salt, mustard,
TABASCO, and bay leaves.

Set the marinade aside.
Place shrimp in the rapidly
boiling seasoned water and
cook for 3 minutes or until
shrimp are bright pink and
cooked. Drain.

Immediately toss the shrimp
in the marinade. Add the
onions. Cover and refrigerate
them for at least 4 hours.
Remove from the refrigerator
just before serving.

Serves: 6 as an appetizer

TIP: Always remove bay
leaves from the finished
recipe. Never try to eat a bay
leaf, because it's indigestable!

PORTOBELLO BURGERS WITH RED PEPPERS AND GORGONZOLA CHEESE

Ingredients:

4 large Portobello mushrooms—stems removed—gills removed
1/4 cup Heinz® Balsamic Vinegar
3 garlic cloves—minced + 1 whole garlic clove—peeled and halved
1 tablespoon chopped fresh thyme
1/4 cup extra virgin olive oil + more for brushing
2 red bell peppers—roasted and cut into thin strips
Kosher salt and freshly ground black pepper to taste
1/2–3/4 cup crumbled gorgonzola cheese
8 1/2-inch-thick slices rustic country bread cut from a 6-inch-high loaf
1/2 cup mayonnaise
1/2 cup shredded fresh basil

Directions:

Clean the Portobello caps. Combine 3 tablespoons of vinegar with the minced garlic, thyme and 1/4 cup of olive oil in a small bowl. Divide the mixture between 2 large, resealable plastic bags. Put 2 mushrooms in each bag and seal. Marinate the mushrooms at room temperature for 1 hour, turning the bags often.

Season the roasted peppers with salt and pepper to taste. Grill the mushrooms on a preheated grill at a medium-high temperature, cap sides up, for about 4–5 minutes or until they are softened. When they are almost done grilling, sprinkle an equal amount of the cheese into the cavity of each cap.

PORTOBELLO BURGERS WITH RED PEPPERS AND GORGONZOLA CHEESE

While the mushrooms are grilling, brush the bread with the olive oil on both sides. Grill the bread until lightly toasted. Rub one side of each slice with the cut garlic clove while hot.

Add the reserved tablespoon of vinegar to the mayonnaise. Stir well and season with the salt and pepper. Spread on the same side as the garlic clove. Top half the bread slices with a mushroom cap and equal amounts of peppers and basil. Place the other slice of bread on top and cut the burgers into halves and serve immediately.

Serves: 4

TIP: Never soak mushrooms in water to clean them, because they're like sponges and will become very soggy. Simply wet a paper towel and wipe off any dirt on the mushroom.

LOBSTER COCKTAIL A LA RITZ

Ingredients:

12 ounces cooked lobster meat
1 celery heart—diced
1 lettuce heart—chopped
1/2 cup good quality mayonnaise
2 tablespoons chopped chives
2 tablespoons chopped parsley
1 tomato—seeded, peeled and chopped
1 tablespoon Heinz® Worcestershire Sauce
2 tablespoons Heinz® Seafood Cocktail Sauce
Lemon wedges for garnish

Directions:

Make a dressing with all the ingredients except the lobster meat.

Combine with the lobster and serve in stemmed goblets.

Garnish with lemon wedges.

Serves: 4

TIP: On a budget? Substitute langoustines (Chilean lobster) for the lobster meat in this recipe, which you can purchase in the seafood freezer section of your local grocery store.

CRAB LOUIS

Ingredients:
1 cup mayonnaise
1/3 cup Heinz® Chili Sauce
1/4 cup minced scallion
2 tablespoons minced green olives
2 teaspoons fresh lemon juice
2 teaspoons Heinz® Worcestershire Sauce
1 teaspoon (drained and squeezed dry) bottled horseradish
1-1/2 pounds jumbo lump crabmeat, picked over
Boston Bibb lettuce

Garnish:
Capers
Tomato wedges
Hard-boiled egg quarters
Lemon wedges

Directions:
Whisk together mayonnaise, chili sauce, scallion, olives, lemon juice, worcestershire sauce, horseradish, and salt and pepper to taste in a bowl.

Divide crabmeat among 4 plates lined with lettuce leaves.

Top with garnishes and serve with dressing.

TIP: When slicing a hard-boiled egg, wet the knife just before cutting.

GRILLED GARLIC AND HERB CHICKEN SALAD

Ingredients:
Grilled garlic and herb chicken:
1 Jack Daniel's® Slow Roasted Garlic and Herb EZ Marinader® bag
1-1/2 pounds boneless chicken breasts—halved and skin removed

Salad:
1/4 cup freshly squeezed lemon juice
1/4 cup extra virgin olive oil
1 cup snow peas—blanched just until crisp tender
1/2 cup red bell pepper—julienned
1/2 cup yellow bell pepper—julienned
1 lemon thinly sliced
Kosher salt and freshly ground black pepper to taste

Directions:
Place the chicken in the Jack Daniel's Slow Roasted Garlic and Herb EZ Marinader bag. Marinate the chicken, following the package directions.

Heat a charcoal grill and cook the chicken breasts for 6 minutes on each side, or until just cooked through. Cool slightly and cut diagonally in 3/8-inch-thick slices. Chill until ready to assemble the salad.

Salad: Toss the chilled chicken slices along with any reserved juices with the lemon juice, olive oil, snow peas, red and yellow bell peppers, lemon slices, and salt and pepper to taste.

Taste for seasoning and serve cold.

Serves: 4

TIP: When preparing dishes such as chicken or cooked meat salads, use chilled ingredients. Make sure cooked chicken has been cooked and chilled before mixing it with other salad ingredients.

TOMATO AND BREAD SALAD WITH BASIL AND RED ONION

Ingredients:

8 ounces stale Italian bread
—cut into 2-inch pieces
8 cups cold water
2 pounds ripe tomatoes—
coarsely chopped
(about 5 cups)
I small red onion—thinly
sliced
I cup (loosely packed) fresh
basil leaves—torn into
bite-sized pieces
1/3 cup Heinz® Red Wine
Vinegar
1/2 cup extra virgin olive oil
Kosher salt and fresh-ground
black pepper to taste

Directions:

Place bread in large bowl.
Pour in enough cold water
(about 8 cups) to cover
bread. Soak 5 minutes.
Drain well, squeeze bread to
remove as much liquid as
possible. Coarsely crumble
bread into same bowl. Add
tomatoes, onion and basil.
Pour vinegar into small
bowl. Gradually whisk in
oil. Season vinaigrette to
taste with salt and pepper.
Toss salad with enough
vinaigrette to coat. Season
generously with salt and
pepper.

Can be prepared 8 hours
ahead. Cover and chill.
Let stand I hour at room
temperature before serving.

Serves: 4

TIP: This is great recipe
that uses up stale bread.
However, to keep bread
fresh longer, place a celery
rib in the bread package
when storing.

GRILLED PITTSBURGH STEAK SALAD WITH CHEDDAR FRIES

Ingredients:

2 12-ounce New York strip steaks
Heinz® 57 Sauce for basting steak
6 cups romaine lettuce—torn into bite-sized pieces
1 cup shredded carrots
1 English cucumber—sliced
1/2 cup chickpeas
6 radishes—sliced
1 cup cherry tomatoes—cut into halves
1 small, red Bermuda onion—sliced
Good quality bottled Italian dressing
1 bag Ore-Ida® Extra Crispy™ Golden Crinkles—baked according to package directions
Shredded cheddar cheese

Directions:

Preheat your grill to a medium-high heat. Season the steak with salt and pepper to taste. Grill the steak about 5 minutes per side, until medium-rare, basting often with the Heinz 57 Sauce.

Remove steak to a cutting board and let stand 10 minutes before cutting into slices.

Combine the lettuce, carrots, cucumber, chickpeas, radishes, cherry tomatoes, and red Bermuda onion in a large salad bowl. Dress the salad with your favorite bottled Italian dressing. Fan the steak slices on top of the salad and top the salad with the Ore-Ida Crispy Fries. They make great croutons! Sprinkle a generous amount of shredded cheddar cheese over the hot fries and serve immediately.

Serves: 4

TIP: To remove that "starchy" taste from chickpeas, always drain and rinse twice before adding them to the salad.

ORZO SALAD WITH FETA AND BLACK OLIVES

Ingredients:
Dressing:
1/4 cup Heinz® Red Wine
   Vinegar
3/4 cup extra virgin olive oil
1/4 cup minced fresh parsley
1/4 cup minced fresh basil
Salt and freshly ground black
   pepper to taste

Salad:
1 pound uncooked orzo
1-1/2 pints cherry
   tomatoes—halved
1 cup pitted Kalamata olives
   —coarsely chopped
1/2 cup chopped green
   onions
1 cup (or to taste) crumbled
   feta cheese

Directions:
For dressing: In a small
bowl, whisk the dressing
ingredients together. This is
not an emulsified dressing—
so it won't hold together.

For salad: Cook the orzo in
rapidly boiling, salted water
until tender, for about 7–10
minutes or according to
package instructions. Drain
well and toss with a little
extra virgin olive oil. Allow
the orzo to cool.

To finish: Combine the
cooled orzo with the
dressing and the remaining
salad ingredients.

Serves: 8

TIP: To pit Kalamata
olives easily, place them on
a cutting board and, with the
flat side of a large chopping
knife, press down on the
olive to flatten it. The pit
will slide right out!

PASTA E FAGIOLI

Ingredients:

2 cups dried cranberry or cannellini beans
5 cups cold water
3 tablespoons olive oil
1/4 pound pancetta—finely chopped
4 large garlic cloves—finely chopped
2 large carrots—peeled and finely chopped
2 large celery ribs—finely chopped
1 large onion—finely chopped
1–2 cups canned diced plum tomatoes
8 cups chicken stock made from Wyler's® Chicken Bouillon
Salt and freshly ground black pepper to taste
1/2 pound small pasta shells—cooked al dente
Extra virgin olive oil
Freshly grated Asiago cheese

Directions:

Put the beans in a large saucepan and add the cold water.
Bring the water to a boil over high heat; reduce the heat to
medium and simmer for about 5 minutes. Turn off the heat
and leave the beans to sit for 1 hour. Drain them and set
them aside.

PASTA E FAGIOLI

In a the soup pot, heat the olive oil over medium heat. Add the pancetta and cook, stirring frequently, for 5 minutes. Add the garlic, carrots, celery, and onion and cook, stirring, for 5 minutes longer. Add the beans, tomatoes, Wyler's chicken stock, and 2 teaspoons of salt. Bring to a boil, then reduce the heat and simmer, covered, until the beans are tender, about 1 hour. Season to taste with salt and pepper.

Add the cooked pasta shells to the soup and simmer for a few minutes longer.

Ladle the soup into bowls and top with a swirl of extra virgin olive oil, some grated Asiago cheese, and a liberal grinding of black pepper. Serve immediately.

Serves: 6 as a main course

TIP: Serve this wonderful, heart-warming soup at your next tailgating party by taking it to the stadium in a large thermos. Make sure you take lots of rustic Italian bread to go with your soup!

SEAFOOD SALAD

Ingredients:

For the seafood:
1/2 cup Heinz® Tarragon Vinegar
1 tablespoon kosher salt
1-1/2 pounds large shrimp—peeled and deveined
1 pound sea scallops
1 pound jumbo lump crabmeat

For the sauce:
1 cup extra virgin olive oil
1/2 teaspoon whole fresh tarragon leaves
2 teaspoons minced garlic
Zest of 2 lemons
1/4 cup freshly squeezed lemon juice
1 teaspoon Heinz® Spicy Brown Mustard or more to taste
2 tablespoons Heinz® Tarragon Vinegar
Salt and freshly ground black pepper to taste

To assemble:
1 cup medium diced celery
4 tablespoons chopped fresh parsley
Thinly sliced lemon—for garnish

Directions:

To cook the seafood: Combine 8 cups of boiling water with the tarragon vinegar and salt in a large pot, and bring to a boil. Add the shrimp and cook for about 2–3 minutes. Remove with a slotted spoon and set aside. Bring the water back to a boil and cook the scallops for 4 minutes or until just cooked through. Drain.

SEAFOOD SALAD

Drain all the cooked seafood and place it in a large bowl with the jumbo lump crabmeat, being careful not to break up the crab too much.

To make the sauce: Heat the olive oil in a medium sauté pan and add the thyme, garlic and lemon zest. Cook over low heat for I minute. Off the heat, add the lemon juice, mustard, vinegar, and salt and pepper. Pour the hot vinaigrette over the seafood.

Add the celery and parsley, and toss well. This salad can be served immediately, but it is best when refrigerated for an hour or two. Sprinkle with salt and toss with sliced lemon.

Serves: 6

TIP: When chopping fresh herbs, hold them together in small bunches and snip with kitchen scissors. It's fast, and you'll find the herbs will be light and fluffy, not bruised and wet as they often get when chopped.

TERIYAKI STEAK AND BASMATI RICE SALAD

Ingredients:
1 Jack Daniel's® Honey Teriyaki EZ Marinader® bag
1 pound sirloin steak (3/4-inch-thick piece)

Salad:
3/4 cup basmati rice
1-1/2 cups water
1 cup snow peas
3/4 cup diced red bell pepper
3/4 cup grated carrots
1/4 cup chopped green onions

Directions:
Open the EZ Marinader bag and pour off about 1/2 cup of the marinade and reserve for the salad.

Place the steak in the EZ Marinader bag. Marinate the steak, following the package directions.

Meanwhile, combine the rice and water in a medium saucepan. Cover and bring to a simmer. Reduce heat to low and simmer for 12 minutes.

Add peas and cook for a few minutes or until rice is tender and liquid has been absorbed. Place in a large, shallow bowl; fluff with a fork and cool slightly. Add bell pepper, carrots and green onions. Drizzle salad with reserved marinade and toss to coat.

Heat grill to medium-high heat. Remove steak from marinader bag and discard remaining marinade. Grill steak 6–8 minutes until medium-rare or to desired doneness. Let stand for 10 minutes. Thinly slice across the grain and place on salad.

Serves: 4

TIP: Because there's sugar in all BBQ sauces and marinades, they tend to burn easily when grilling. So watch meat carefully and turn it often to minimize burning.

SWEET VICTORY CRAB CHOWDER

Ingredients:

2 tablespoons olive oil
1/4 cup chopped tasso
    (about 2 ounces)
1/4 cup chopped shallots
2 cloves garlic—minced
2 cups peeled sweet
    potatoes—1/2-inch
    diced
2 cups chicken stock made
    from Wyler's® Chicken
    Bouillon
1 cup heavy cream
2 cups milk
2 tablespoons flour
1 pound crabmeat—picked
    over for shells and
    cartilage
3 tablespoons chopped
    chives
Salt and freshly ground black
    pepper to taste

Directions:

In a large soup pot over
medium heat, heat the oil.
Add the tasso and cook,
stirring for 1 minute. Add
the shallots and cook for 3
minutes. Add the garlic,
sweet potatoes and broth,
and bring to a boil.

Cover and cook for 15
minutes or until the potatoes
are tender. In a medium
bowl, whisk together the
cream, milk and flour. Add
to the soup and cook until
the mixture begins to
thicken. Add the crabmeat
and the chives. Season with
the salt and pepper to taste.

Serves: 4

TIP: Shallots burn easily
because of their high sugar
content. For this reason,
sauté briefly over low-to-
medium heat. Shallots will
keep for approximately six
months if stored in a cool,
dry location.

DO AHEAD BARBECUED CHICKEN

Ingredients:

1/2 cup freshly squeezed orange juice
1 shallot—finely chopped
1 tablespoon Heinz® Spicy Brown Mustard
Coarse salt and freshly ground black pepper to taste
2 frying chickens—about 3 pounds each—cut into pieces
1 cup Jack Daniel's® Original No. 7 Recipe™ Barbecue Sauce

Directions:

In a small bowl, combine the orange juice, shallot, mustard, and salt and pepper to taste. Arrange the chicken pieces in a large shallow glass dish and pour the marinade over the chicken to coat it well. Cover and refrigerate the chicken for about 2–4 hours.

Preheat the oven to 375 degrees.

Remove the chicken from the marinade and place the chicken in roasting pan large enough to hold the chicken in a single layer. Pour the marinade over the chicken and cover the pan with aluminum foil. Roast the chicken for about 35 minutes, or until the juices run clear. The chicken will be just about cooked through. Remove the chicken from the oven and transfer to a platter. Pour the juices into a bowl and combine them with the Jack Daniel's Barbecue Sauce. Keep both the sauce and the chicken covered and chilled in the refrigerator.

DO AHEAD BARBECUED CHICKEN

When ready to serve, preheat your gas grill to a medium-high heat. In a small pot, heat the barbecue sauce until bubbling and hot. Place the chicken pieces on the rack and grill them, basting with the sauce. Grill the chicken until the skin is crisp and brown. Baste the chicken often with the sauce. The chicken should take about 10–15 minutes to finish cooking. Remove from the grill and serve with the remaining heated sauce on the side.

Serves: 8

TIP: If your oranges are a little hard and without much juice, put them in the microwave for 15 seconds before juicing them.

GRILLED CHICKEN FAJITAS

Ingredients:
Juice of 4 limes
6 tablespoons oil
Salt and freshly ground black
    pepper to taste
1 tablespoon minced fresh
    garlic
1-1/2 pounds skinless,
    boneless chicken breasts
Jack Daniel's® Honey
    Smokehouse Barbecue
    Sauce
4 tablespoons olive oil
2 large onions—sliced
2 packages 6-inch flour
    tortillas
2 cups guacamole—see
    attached recipe
8 ounces sour cream
2 large, ripe tomatoes,
    seeded, peeled, diced
1-1/2 cups pepper Monterey
    Jack cheese—grated
TABASCO® to taste
Chopped parsley

Guacamole:
2 ripe avacados—pitted
    and peeled
2 jalapeño peppers—seeded
    and minced
1 tomato—chopped
3 tablespoons lime juice or
    to taste
2 tablespoons chopped
    onion
1 clove garlic—minced
1/2 teaspoon cumin
1/2 teaspoon salt
1/4 teaspoon pepper

Directions:
Combine first 5 ingredients
and marinate chicken, keep
covered in refrigerator for
2 hours.

In a large skillet, sauté the
onions in the 4 tablespoons
of olive oil. Season with salt
and pepper.

Prepare barbecue grill to
medium-high heat and grill
the chicken breasts until
they are cooked through—
but still moist. You may also
pan grill the chicken using a
nonstick grill pan. During the
last few minutes of your
grilling time, brush the
chicken with lots of Jack
Daniel's Honey Smokehouse
Barbecue Sauce.

GRILLED CHICKEN FAJITAS

Make sure you have a bowl of the sauce to serve with all the other fajita condiments on your tailgating table.

Slice the cooked chicken breasts into strips 3 inches long and 1/2-inch wide.

Lay the 12 tortillas on a large platter and serve along with the chicken, onions, guacamole, sour cream, tomatoes, Jack Daniel's Honey Smokehouse Barbecue Sauce, and cheese. Let each person fill a tortilla according to taste—top with a dash of TABASCO sauce and sprinkle with chopped parsley. Fold and enjoy!

Guacamole Directions:

In a bowl, mash all of the ingredients together with a fork until thoroughly blended and still chunky. You may also use a food processor using on/off turns to make your guacamole. Remove the guacamole to a serving bowl and cover tightly by laying a sheet of plastic wrap directly on the surface of the guacamole and gently squeezing out any air bubbles. Seal the wrap to the edges of the bowl and refrigerate until ready to use.

Serves: 6

TIP: When making guacamole from scratch, always buy avocados that are almost brown in color. The skin of the avocado should not be hard and bright green. It should be a little "wrinkled" in appearance!

OPEN-FACED HOT TURKEY SANDWICHES WITH TURKEY GRAVY

Ingredients:

Stuffing:
1 pound bulk sausage—cooked and drained
1 stick melted, unsalted butter
1 large onion—chopped
3 large celery ribs—diced
10 cups stale bread cubes
1/2 cup parsley—chopped
2 teaspoons sage
2 teaspoons poultry seasoning
Salt and pepper to taste
1 cup chicken stock made from Wyler's® Chicken Bouillion
4 cups of your favorite mashed potatoes
8 strips crisp-cooked bacon—diced

Apple cranberry sauce:
1 cup store-bought apple sauce
1 14-ounce can whole berry cranberry sauce

Turkey and gravy:
2 pounds roasted turkey breast meat
1 jar Heinz® Homestyle Turkey Gravy
8 thick slices whole-grain bread
2 tablespoons chopped chives, for garnish

Directions:

Stuffing: Melt 2 tablespoons of the butter in a skillet and cook the onion and the celery until soft and translucent— about 15 minutes. Scrape the vegetable mixture into a large bowl and add the bread cubes, parsley, sage, poultry seasoning, and salt and pepper. Toss well.

OPEN-FACED HOT TURKEY SANDWICHES WITH TURKEY GRAVY

Add the reserved sausage meat along with the remaining 6 tablespoons of melted butter and toss again. Drizzle the chicken stock over the top and toss lightly. Spoon the stuffing into a greased, 3-quart casserole, and bake covered for 40 minutes at 350 degrees.

Mashed potatoes:
Combine warmed mashed potatoes with crisp bacon—keep warm while finishing the recipe.

Apple cranberry sauce:
Combine the apple sauce and canned cranberry sauce in a small pot and gently heat through, about 10 minutes.

Slice turkey into 16 thick slices.

Heat the turkey gravy in a small pot.

Place a bread slice on dinner plate. Use a large ice cream scoop to place a mound of stuffing on the bread. Place turkey on top of stuffing. Serve mashed potatoes and cranberries on the side. Spoon the gravy over potatoes and turkey sandwiches. Sprinkle the plates with chopped chives and serve.

Serves: 8

TIP: The best bread to use in stuffing is challah bread.

QUESADILLAS WITH CARAMELIZED ONIONS & CHICKEN

Ingredients:

1-1/2 cups shredded, cooked chicken breast
1 tablespoon vegetable oil
2 large red Bermuda onions—thinly sliced
1/2 cup beer
2 tablespoons Heinz® Balsamic Vinegar
2 tablespoons brown sugar
1 jalapeño chile—seeded and finely chopped
Salt and freshly ground black pepper to taste
3 10-inch flour tortillas
1-1/2 cups shredded jack cheese (or use pepper jack cheese)

Garnishes:

Guacamole
Salsa
Sour cream

Directions:

Set the cooked chicken aside. In a large non-aluminum skillet, heat the oil over medium-high heat. Add the onion and sauté until translucent. Add the beer, vinegar, sugar, and jalapeño to the onions and simmer over low heat until almost all of the liquid has evaporated. The onions should be slightly caramelized. Add the salt and pepper. Taste for seasoning and cool.

QUESADILLAS WITH CARAMELIZED ONIONS & CHICKEN

Heat a nonstick grill pan over medium-high heat. Place a tortilla on the pan and spoon 1/2 cup of the onion mixture evenly over one half. Sprinkle with 1/2 cup of the cooked chicken and top evenly with 1/2 cup of the cheese; fold the tortilla in half, pressing down with a spatula.

Cook the quesadilla until lightly browned, then turn over and cook the other side until lightly brown. Place on a cutting board, slice into wedges, and keep warm under foil. Repeat to cook the remaining quesadillas. Arrange on a large serving platter and serve immediately accompanied by the guacamole, salsa and sour cream.

Serves: 6

TIP: The longer and slower you cook your onions, the sweeter they'll taste. Don't rush the process!

SMOKED TURKEY REUBEN SANDWICHES

Ingredients:

Dressing:
3/4 cup good-quality mayonnaise
1/2 cup Heinz® Chili Sauce
3 tablespoons Heinz® Sweet Relish

Sandwiches:
8 slices rye bread
4 tablespoons unsalted butter—room temperature
1/2 pound shredded Swiss cheese
1/2 pound sliced smoked turkey
1 cup well-drained uncooked sauerkraut

Directions:

Dressing: In a small bowl, stir together the mayonnaise, chili sauce and relish. Set aside while making the sandwiches.

Sandwiches: Butter one side of each of the rye bread slices. Turn the bread slices over and spread each slice evenly with the dressing.

Sprinkle the Swiss cheese over four rye bread slices. Lay the turkey over the cheese, dividing evenly. Spread the sauerkraut over the turkey. Top with the remaining bread slices, buttered side out. Press down firmly.

SMOKED TURKEY REUBEN SANDWICHES

Heat a nonstick griddle over medium-high heat. Carefully transfer the sandwiches to the griddle and grill, occasionally pressing down gently. Grill until the underside is golden, and then carefully turn the sandwiches to continue grilling on the other side until golden and the cheese has melted. Flip the sandwiches and grill for just a couple of minutes longer.

Serve with Heinz® Dill Pickles and Heinz® Spicy Brown Mustard.

Serves: 4

TIP: Use low-fat mayonnaise in this recipe for a healthier dressing.

CHICKEN BREASTS WITH SPICY PEANUT SAUCE

Ingredients:
- 4 boneless chicken breast halves
- 4 tablespoons soy sauce
- 1 tablespoon sesame oil
- 2 teaspoons minced fresh ginger

Sauce:
- 3/4 cup chunky peanut butter
- 1 cup chicken broth made from Wyler's® Chicken Bouillion
- 2 tablespoons brown sugar
- 2 tablespoons soy sauce
- 1 tablespoon minced fresh ginger
- 2 teaspoons chili paste with garlic
- 4 green onions—chopped

Directions:
Place chicken in small baking pan. Pour in soy sauce and oil. Sprinkle chicken with ginger. Turn to coat. Let stand 20 minutes.

Heat grill to medium-high heat.

Grill chicken until just cooked through—about 4 minutes per side.

Prepare sauce: Combine peanut butter, broth, sugar, soy sauce, ginger, and chili paste in a heavy small saucepan. Simmer sauce until smooth and slightly thickened, whisking frequently, about 4 minutes.

Arrange chicken on platter. Spoon sauce over chicken. Sprinkle with sliced green onions.

Serve immediately.

Serves: 4

TIP: When grilling boneless and skinless chicken breasts, just cook through until juices run clear. Never overcook chicken, because it dries out and becomes very tough.

CHILI CHEESE DOGS

Ingredients:

1/4 cup extra virgin olive oil
1 medium onion—chopped
1 pound lean ground beef
1 cup Heinz® Ketchup
1 teaspoon chili powder
1 tablespoon Heinz® Yellow
   Mustard
Kosher salt and freshly
   ground pepper
4 all-beef hot dogs—4
   ounces each
4 top-sliced hot dog rolls
1 cup shredded cheddar
   cheese

Directions:

To make the chili: Heat a skillet over medium flame and add 2 tablespoons of olive oil. Add the onion and cook, stirring, until soft and translucent, about 5 minutes. Add the ground beef, breaking it up with the back of a spoon, and cook until nicely browned, about 10 minutes. Stir in the ketchup, chili powder and mustard; simmer for 15 minutes until thick; season with salt and pepper.

For the hot dogs: While the chili is cooking, preheat an outdoor gas grill to a medium-high heat. Brush the grate with oil to keep the hot dogs from sticking.

Parboil the dogs first before grilling: Bring a pot of water to a boil and cook the hot dogs for about 5 minutes. Remove from the water and grill the hot dogs just long enough to give them grill marks. Brush the insides of the rolls with the remaining oil and place them face down on the grill until lightly browned and toasted.

To serve: Top each hot dog with the chili and some cheddar cheese.

TIP: Parboiling hotdogs prior to grilling results in much juicier and plumper hot dogs that burst with flavor.

BEEF TENDERLOIN STEAKS WITH GORGONZOLA AND MUSHROOMS

Ingredients:

4 1-1/2-inch-thick beef
    tenderloin steaks
1 tablespoon extra virgin
    olive oil
Salt and freshly ground black
    pepper
3/4 pound gorgonzola
    cheese
1/2 bunch fresh basil leaves
    —julienned
1 jar Heinz® Homestyle Beef
    Gravy
Mushroom sauté (see recipe
    below)

Directions:

Place a large, flat griddle
over high heat. When hot,
using a pair of tongs and a
folded paper towel, wipe
cooking surface with oil
and place steaks on hot
griddle. Sear the steaks,
2 minutes on each side.
Reduce heat to moderate.
Season meat with salt and
pepper and cook 4 to 5
minutes longer on each side.

In a small pot, heat the
Heinz Homestyle Gravy until
hot and just beginning to
bubble.

Preheat broiler to high.

Arrange steaks on baking
sheet. Top each steak with 3
ounces gorgonzola. Place on
baking sheet 6 inches from
broiler and heat just long
enough to melt the cheese.
Remove meat from the oven
and top with slivers of fresh
basil. Let meat rest 2 or 3
minutes, then serve
immediately with the Heinz
Homestyle Gravy and
mushroom sauté.

Serves: 4

Mushroom sauté:

1 pound mixed mushrooms,
    such as shiitake, cremini,
    or white button
2 to 4 tablespoons unsalted
    butter
1 medium shallot or 1/2
    small onion—chopped

BEEF TENDERLOIN STEAKS WITH GORGONZOLA AND MUSHROOMS

1/2 teaspoon kosher salt
Freshly ground black pepper
3 sprigs fresh thyme, leaves
  stripped
1/2 cup Madeira wine

Directions:

Clean the mushrooms by brushing with a kitchen towel or a brush to remove any loose dirt. Remove the shiitake stems and discard. Trim the dry ends off the cremini and white mushroom stems. Quarter all the mushrooms and put in a bowl.

Heat 2 tablespoons of the butter in a large skillet over medium-high heat. Add the mushrooms and spread them out evenly in the pan, increase the heat to high. Let the mushrooms cook until they brown. Shake the pan to turn them over. Add the additional butter along the sides of the pan as the mushrooms cook if the pan seems too dry. Continue to

cook until nicely browned, about 5 minutes. Add the shallot and cook until softened, about 2 minutes. Season the mushrooms with the salt and pepper, and add the thyme. Pull the pan off the heat and add the Madeira. Return pan to the heat and scrape up any of the brown bits that cling to the bottom of the pan with a wooden spoon. Remove from the heat and serve with the steaks.

Yields: 2 cups

TIP: Store freshly cut basil at room temperature in a glass with water covering only the stems. Change the water occasionally. It'll keep for weeks and ultimately develop roots. Basil doesn't like the cold, so never put in the refrigerator. Also, regular cutting encourages new growth and healthy plants.

BEER-SIMMERED BRATWURST WITH GRILLED ONIONS AND SAUERKRAUT

Ingredients:

For the sauerkraut:

2 cups Heinz® Red Wine Vinegar
I cup water
1/4 cup sugar
I large head red cabbage—cored and thinly shredded
2 cloves garlic—thinly sliced
I teaspoon whole mustard seeds
Salt and freshly ground pepper

For the bratwurst:

3 large onions—thinly sliced
3 pounds precooked bratwurst—pricked with a fork
6 12-ounce bottles dark beer
2 cups water
I teaspoon coriander seeds
I teaspoon caraway seeds
I teaspoon mustard seeds
I 1-inch piece fresh ginger—peeled and chopped
Hot dog buns, hoagie buns, or bratwurst buns
Heinz® Spicy Brown Mustard

Directions:

For the sauerkraut: Combine the vinegar, water and sugar in a large saucepan (not aluminum or cast iron); bring to a boil, reduce the heat, and simmer until the sugar has dissolved. Add the remaining ingredients and simmer until the cabbage is soft, about 20 minutes. Season to taste with salt and pepper. (The sauerkraut can be made up to 2 days in advance, cooled, covered, and kept refrigerated. Bring to room temperature and drain before serving.)

BEER-SIMMERED BRATWURST WITH GRILLED ONIONS AND SAUERKRAUT

For the bratwurst: Arrange the onion slices on the bottom of a medium stock pot. Place the bratwurst on top and add the beer, water, coriander, caraway, mustard seeds, and ginger. Bring to a simmer and cook for about 10 minutes. Remove from the heat and set aside for at least 10 minutes and up to 1 hour.

When ready to serve, heat grill to high. Lift the sausages out of the pot. Remove the onions with a slotted spoon and place in a serving bowl. Discard the remaining liquid and aromatics. Grill the sausages until crisp and golden brown on all sides, about 10 minutes total. If you like, grill the buns until lightly toasted.

Serve the bratwurst on the buns with sauerkraut, onions and mustard.

TIP: Always use fresh ginger—never dried! It makes all the difference in this recipe!

HOT AND SWEET KIELBASA

Ingredients:
2 pounds kielbasa—cut into
   2-inch chunks

**Hot and sweet
barbecue sauce:**
1/4 cup Heinz® Apple Cider
   Vinegar
2 tablespoons Heinz® 57
   Sauce
2 teaspoons chili powder
1 jar orange marmalade
1-1/3 cups Heinz® Ketchup

Directions:
To make the BBQ sauce:
In a small saucepan,
combine all of the sauce
ingredients. Heat and stir
until blended.

Preheat the grill to medium-
high heat. Grill the kielbasa,
turning several times, until it
starts to brown. Brush the
hot and sweet BBQ sauce
over the kielbasa during the
last few minutes of grilling.

Serve the grilled kielbasa
with lots of toothpicks and
extra sauce for dipping!

**Serves: 2 hungry
Steelers fans or 8
regular fans...**

TIP: Watching your fat
intake? Trying substituting
turkey kielbasa for the beef
kielbasa in this recipe.

RANIA'S MEATLOAF

Ingredients:
2 pounds lean ground beef
4 tablespoons unsalted
    butter
1 large onion—chopped
2 eggs
4 slices whole-wheat
    bread—toasted (crusts
    removed)
1-1/2 cups tomato sauce
Salt and pepper to taste
2 teaspoons oregano
1/2 cup chopped fresh
    parsley
Garlic mashed potatoes
1 jar Heinz® Homestyle Beef
    Gravy

Directions:
Place the ground beef in a large bowl and set aside.

Melt the butter in a small skillet and sauté the onions until lightly golden in color. Add the cooked onions to the ground beef. Add the eggs, toasted whole-wheat bread and enough tomato sauce to make the mixture light—yet firm enough to hold together when shaping into your loaf.

Season with salt, pepper and oregano. Blend in the chopped parsley and knead the mixture gently until all ingredients are well combined.

Coat a 9 x 13-inch pan with nonstick spray and form the mixture into an oval loaf. Bake in a preheated 350-degree oven until cooked through and nicely browned —about 1 hour. Serve immediately with garlic mashed potatoes and Heinz Homestyle Gravy.

Serves: 6–8

TIP: Sauté onions before adding them to the meatloaf mixture, to soften and sweeten, so they won't leave a strong aftertaste. Uncooked onions will remain crunchy, and take on a very strong onion-like flavor in the meatloaf.

PEPPER-CRUSTED RIB-EYE STEAKS WITH BARBECUED RED ONIONS
AND TEXAS GARLIC TOAST

Ingredients:

Rib-eye steaks:
4 bone-in rib-eye steaks (about 12 ounces each)
Olive oil
Salt to taste
1/4 cup ancho chile powder
1/4 cup freshly ground black pepper

Barbecued red onions:
2 large red Bermuda onions—sliced 1/2-inch thick
1 cup Jack Daniel's® Honey Smokehouse Barbecue Sauce
Coarse salt and freshly ground black pepper to taste

Texas toast:
2 sticks unsalted butter—softened
4 cloves roasted garlic—mashed to a paste
Salt and pepper
1 loaf good-quality white bread—sliced 1-inch thick

Directions:

Rib-eye steaks: Preheat your grill to a medium-high heat. Brush the steaks with olive oil and season with salt. Mix the ancho chile powder and the black pepper together in a small bowl. Dredge the steaks with the pepper mixture on one side and grill them pepper side down for 4–5 minutes or until they turn golden brown. Turn the steaks over and continue grilling them for another 5 minutes or until they are cooked to a medium-rare doneness.

PEPPER-CRUSTED RIB-EYE STEAKS WITH BARBECUED RED ONIONS
AND TEXAS GARLIC TOAST

Barbecued red onions: Brush the onion slices with the Jack Daniel's Grilling Sauce and season them with salt and pepper to taste. Grill them on both sides until they begin to caramelize and are just about cooked through.

Texas garlic toast: Mix together the butter and roasted garlic, and season the mixture with salt and pepper to taste. Spread the butter on one side of the bread and grill, buttered side down, until toasted and golden brown.

Serve the steaks with Jack Daniel's® Steak Sauce and Ore-Ida® Extra Crispy™ Golden Crinkles with Heinz® Ketchup.

Serves: 4

TIP: Whenever barbecuing, use tongs to turn the meat. A fork punches holes in the meat, and allows the natural juices to escape. The steak will lose its flavor and become tough and chewy.

THE BURGER BAR

Ingredients:
Grilled turkey burgers
Grilled beef burgers

For the onions:
4 1/2-inch-thick slices red onion
Jack Daniel's® Honey Smokehouse Barbecue Sauce

Topping for burgers:
Heinz® Hot and Spicy Ketchup Kick'rs®
Sliced Monterey pepper jack cheese
Guacamole
Your favorite chunky salsa
Heinz® Dill Pickles
Ore-Ida® Extra Crispy™ Golden Crinkles
Your favorite Heinz® Ketchup

Chipotle mayonnaise:
1/2 cup mayonnaise
1 teaspoon sugar
1 tablespoon puréed chipotle in adobo sauce (from canned
    chipotles) or to taste
Juice of 1/2 lime
Sesame seed and whole-wheat hamburger buns—toasted

Directions:
Preheat barbecue to a medium-high heat.

For the burgers: Shape the ground turkey and the ground beef into 4 patties each, about 3/4-inch thick. Season with salt and pepper to taste.

THE BURGER BAR

Coat the turkey burgers with a nonstick spray before grilling so they won't stick to the grill grate. Grill the burgers until they are cooked all the way through, but be careful not to dry them out.

Meanwhile, grill the onions while the burgers are cooking—brushing with the Jack Daniel's Sauce. Grill the onions until soft—about 8 minutes. Turn often, brushing with additional sauce.

For the chipotle mayonnaise: Blend all of the ingredients together in a small bowl and allow to sit for about 30 minutes before serving.

Serve the burgers with the Heinz Hot and Spicy Ketchup Kick'rs, jack cheese, guacamole, salsa, Heinz Dill Pickles, and chipotle mayonnaise; along with the grilled onions and plenty of Ore-Ida Extra Crispy Golden Crinkles!

Serves: 8

TIP: Whenever you empty a jar of dill pickles, use the leftover juice to clean the copper bottoms of your pans. Just pour the juice in a large bowl, set the pan in the juice for about 15 minutes, and your pan will come out looking like new!

BEER-MARINATED GRILLED STEAK

Ingredients:

Marinade:

12 ounces lager-style beer
1/2 cup soy sauce
1/4 cup Heinz® Apple Cider
    Vinegar
1/4 cup Heinz® Ketchup
2 tablespoons Heinz® Spicy
    Brown Mustard
2 tablespoons minced garlic
1 tablespoon Heinz®
    Worcestershire Sauce
1 tablespoon TABASCO®
1/4 cup extra virgin olive oil
Salt and freshly ground black
    pepper to taste

Steak:

2-1/2 pounds boneless
    New York strip, rib-eye,
    or sirloin steak (1-1/2
    inches thick)

Ore-Ida® French Fries and
    Heinz® Ketchup

Directions:

Place steak in a large,
resealable plastic bag. In a
small bowl, stir together all
marinade ingredients and
pour over steak.

Seal bag. Refrigerate
overnight, turning bag
occasionally.

Preheat grill to medium-
high heat. Remove steak
from marinade and discard
marinade. Place steak on
grill for about 10 minutes
until medium-rare or desired
doneness, turning once.

Place on cutting board and
allow the meat to rest for 5
minutes. Slice and serve
with Ore-Ida French Fries
and Heinz Ketchup.

Serves: 4

TIP: Always grill cold meat.
Never allow it to rest at
room temperature prior to
grilling because of food
safety. The other reason is
that the natural juices will
remain in the meat, resulting
in a juicier end product.

GRILLED SWEET AND HOT SAUSAGE HOAGIES

Ingredients:

3 red onions—sliced in half
3 tablespoons olive oil
Salt and freshly ground
  pepper
I clove garlic—finely chopped
I small jalapeño pepper—
  finely diced
I cup Heinz® Red Wine
  Vinegar
1/4 cup creme de cassis
1/4 cup grenadine
1/4 cup red wine
1/4 cup parsley—coarsely
  chopped
2 red peppers—grilled,
  quartered and seeded
I pound hot Italian sausage
I pound sweet Italian
  sausage
4 hoagie rolls
Ore-Ida® Extra Crispy
  Easy Fries™
Heinz® Easy Squeeze™
  Ketchup

Directions:

Preheat grill. Brush the
onions with I tablespoon of
the olive oil and season with
salt and pepper, and grill
until lightly brown. Remove
from the grill and slice thinly.
Heat the remaining olive oil
in a medium saucepan over
medium heat. Add the
onions, garlic and jalapeño,
and cook for I minute.
Add the vinegar, cassis,
grenadine, and red wine and
reduce until the liquid has
almost evaporated to make
a marmalade. Remove from
heat; add the parsley and
salt and pepper to taste.

Grill sausages. Each
sandwich gets sausage,
red pepper and marmalade
on a hoagie roll.

Serve the hoagies with
Ore-Ida Extra Crispy Easy
Fries and Heinz Easy
Squeeze Ketchup to
complete your feast!

Yields: 4 hoagies

TIP: Brush your hoagie
rolls with a little bit of butter
and grill them just before
building the sausage
hoagies.

BARBECUE PORK BURGERS WITH COLESLAW

Ingredients:

Sauce:

3 tablespoons unsalted butter
I cup minced onion
I tablespoon minced garlic
I 1/2 cups Heinz® Ketchup
5 tablespoons Heinz®
    Worcestershire Sauce
I tablespoon dry mustard
1/3 cup Heinz® Apple Cider
    Vinegar
1/3 cup packed brown sugar
I tablespoon chili powder
I teaspoon TABASCO® sauce

Pork burgers:

2 pounds ground pork
1/4 cup fresh breadcrumbs
3 cups coleslaw
6 sesame hamburger buns
Ore-Ida® Zesty' Fries® with
    Heinz® Ketchup Kick'rs®
Heinz® Dill Pickles

Directions:

Sauce: Melt the butter in a sauce pot. Sauté the onions and the garlic until softened. Add the remaining sauce ingredients and simmer for about 15 minutes, stirring the sauce occasionally.

Transfer the sauce to a bowl and cool.

Burgers: Combine the ground pork with the breadcrumbs and 1/2 cup of the sauce, and form into 6 patties. Season the burgers with salt and pepper.

Preheat the grill to a medium-high heat. Grill the burgers on an oiled rack, basting often with remaining sauce and turning several times, until just cooked through. They should cook for about 6–8 minutes per side or until the burgers are no longer pink. Transfer the burgers to the buns.

Top with the coleslaw and serve with the Ore-Ida Zesty Fries and Ketchup Kick'rs with Heinz Dill Pickles on the side.

Serves: 6

TIP: If your brown sugar is hard and a bit dry, microwave it for a few seconds to make it soft and easier to measure.

FOURTH OF JULY BARBECUED RIBS

Ingredients:

4 tablespoons vegetable oil
2 large onions—thinly sliced
1 tablespoon dried thyme
1 cup bourbon
2 cups Jack Daniel's® Honey Smokehouse Barbecue Sauce
4 baby back rib racks—cut into halves

Directions:

For sauce: Sauté the onions in the vegetable oil until they begin to soften. Add the thyme and bourbon and simmer until the mixture is reduced to a glaze. Mix in the Jack Daniel's Grilling Sauce and bring to a boil.

Season the ribs with salt and pepper. Roast them in a 350-degree oven on a rack. Do not cover the ribs. Turn them once and cook them until they are tender and almost cooked through, about 45–60 minutes.

When ready to serve—preheat your grill to a medium-high heat. Put the rib rack halves on the grill and brush them with the barbecue sauce. Grill them until they are well-glazed and browned. Serve the remaining sauce alongside the ribs.

Serves: 4

TIP: For a slightly sweeter sauce, try using Vidalia onions in this recipe.

GINGERED HONEY-SOY PORK TENDERLOIN

Ingredients:

2 pork tenderloins—about
   3/4 pound each
1/3 cup honey
1/4 cup soy sauce
1/4 cup oyster sauce
2 tablespoons brown sugar
1 generous tablespoon fresh
   ginger root—minced
   and peeled
2 tablespoons Heinz®
   Ketchup
1/4 teaspoon garlic powder
1/4 teaspoon cayenne
   pepper
1/4 teaspoon cinnamon

Directions:

Place the pork in a shallow glass baking dish. Whisk all the remaining ingredients together in a bowl and then pour the mixture over the pork. Turn the pork to coat well and cover the dish with plastic wrap. Refrigerate the pork for 12 hours or up to 24 hours. Turn the pork once or twice during the marinating process.

Preheat your grill to a medium-high heat. Remove the pork from the marinade, and save it. Grill the pork on a lightly oiled rack, basting and turning the pork with the reserved marinade every few minutes, for about 10 minutes. Check the internal temperature of the pork with a meat thermometer and make sure that it reaches an internal temperature of 150 degrees. Let the pork stand for 5 minutes before slicing.

Serves: 4–6

TIP: Spray your measuring cup with a little nonstick spray before measuring honey, so it pours out of the cup more easily.

HONEY MUSTARD HAM WITH ORANGE ALMOND SAUCE

Ingredients:
1 6–8 pound ham
1/2 cup honey
1/2 cup Heinz® Spicy Brown Mustard
1/4 teaspoon ground cloves
3 tablespoons dark rum

Orange almond sauce:
2 12-ounce jars of sweet orange marmalade
1/2 cup Heinz® 57 Sauce
1/4 cup minced onion
4 teaspoons fresh-squeezed lemon juice
2 teaspoons soy sauce
1/2 teaspoon ginger
1/4 teaspoon red pepper
1/4 teaspoon allspice
1/2 cup sliced almonds

Directions:
For the ham: Preheat the oven to 325 degrees. Place the ham, fat side up, in a roasting pan. Pour 1-inch of water into the pan. Place the pan in the oven and roast for 1-1/2 hours.

Meanwhile, stir the honey, mustard, cloves, and rum together in a small bowl until smooth. Set aside. Remove the roasting pan from the oven and brush a generous amount of the glaze all over the pan. Roast, brushing a bit more glaze over the ham every 10 minutes or so, until the crust is golden brown and bubbly, another 30 minutes. Slice and serve with the orange almond sauce.

Orange almond sauce:
Combine all of the sauce ingredients except for the sliced almonds in a small saucepan and cook over medium-low heat for 10 minutes or until hot, stirring occasionally. Stir in the almonds. Serve with the honey mustard ham.

Serves: 10–12

TIP: Lemons stored in a sealed jar of water will produce twice the juice.

HONEY TERIYAKI PORK SKEWERS WITH PEANUT SAUCE

Ingredients:

Pork skewers:
2 pork tenderloins—about
    3/4 pound each
Jack Daniel's® Honey Teriyaki
    EZ Marinader® bag

Peanut sauce:
1 cup chunky peanut butter
1-1/2 cups coconut milk
2 tablespoons soy sauce
2 tablespoons honey
1 tablespoon fresh ginger—
    peeled and minced
3 cloves of garlic—minced

Directions:

Cut the pork tenderloin into
1-1/2-inch pieces. Thread the
pork onto wooden or metal
skewers and place them in a
shallow glass baking dish.
Pour all but 1/4 cup of the
Jack Daniel's EZ Marinader
over the pork skewers and
turn the skewers to coat the
pork well. Cover and
refrigerate for about 4–6
hours.

Peanut sauce: In a bowl,
whisk all of the peanut sauce
ingredients to combine well.
Chill until ready to serve the
pork.

To grill the pork skewers:
Preheat your grill to a
medium-high heat. Remove
the skewers from the
marinade and discard the
mixture. Grill the pork
skewers, basting with the
reserved 1/4 cup marinade,
for about 5 minutes per side,
until well-browned and
cooked through. Don't
overcook the pork, or it will
dry out. Arrange the skewers
on a platter, and serve with a
bowl of the peanut sauce in
the middle of the platter.

Serves: 6

TIP: Serve this dish with
a coconut rice and grilled
pineapple at your next
Hawaiian Luau.

GEMELLI PASTA WITH SHRIMP, SCALLOPS AND CHILIES

Ingredients:

4 tablespoons extra virgin
   olive oil
I large, red Bermuda
   onion— sliced
4 cloves of garlic—sliced
2 ounces prosciutto—diced
1/2 pound large shrimp
1/2 pound sea scallops
I cup dry white wine
I cup chicken stock
I pinch saffron
2 cups Classico® Cabernet
   Marinara Sauce
I tablespoon hot chili flakes
I pound gemelli pasta—
   cooked al dente
I bunch stemmed Italian
   parsley—chopped
Salt to taste

Directions:

In a large, heavy pot, heat
olive oil over medium-high
heat. Add onion, garlic and
prosciutto, and sauté until
softened. Add shrimp,
scallops, white wine, saffron,
chicken stock, and the
Classico Cabernet Marinara
Sauce. Bring to a boil.

Add cooked gemelli pasta to
pot and heat through. Add
chili flakes and parsley.
Season to taste with salt.

Serve immediately.

Serves: 4

TIP: If your scallops have
a slightly strong odor, soak
them in milk for a few
minutes, then drain and
rinse and proceed with
the recipe.

BAKED PASTA WITH SAUSAGE AND TOMATO PESTO

Ingredients:

Sauce:

1 pound hot Italian sausage, casings removed
1 onion—finely chopped
3 garlic cloves—minced
2 26-ounce jars Classico® Cabernet Marinara Sauce
6 tablespoons basil pesto
Salt and freshly ground black pepper to taste

Pasta:

1 pound penne pasta—cooked al dente
1/2 pound smoked gouda or mozzarella cheese—finely diced
1 cup freshly grated Parmesan cheese
1 6-ounce bag baby spinach leaves

Directions:

Heat a large dutch oven over medium-high heat and add the sausage. Cook, breaking up the meat with a spoon, for about 5 minutes or until it's no longer pink. Add the onion and sauté for 5 minutes, or until softened, stirring frequently. Add the garlic and cook for 1 minute. Add the marinara sauce and reduce the heat to medium. Simmer for 10 minutes or until the sauce begins to thicken. Stir in the pesto, salt and pepper. Taste and adjust the seasonings. Set aside.

BAKED PASTA WITH SAUSAGE AND TOMATO PESTO

Preheat the oven to 375 degrees. Grease a 9 x 13-inch baking dish. Spread a thin layer of the sauce over the bottom of the pan.

In a large bowl, combine the pasta with the remaining sauce, diced cheese, 1/3 cup of the Parmesan cheese and the spinach leaves, mixing well to combine. Spoon the mixture into the prepared pan and sprinkle the remaining 2/3 cup of Parmesan cheese on top.

Bake for about 30 minutes or until the casserole begins to bubble and the cheese is browned.

Serves: 6–8

TIP: Use a good-quality imported penne pasta for best results in this recipe.

IT'S A PIZZA PICASSO PARTY!

Ingredients:

2 cups Contadina® Pizza Sauce
2 cups Classico® Traditional Basil Pesto
2 cups Classico® Sundried Tomato Sauce
8 ounces diced roasted red peppers
8 ounces diced marinated artichokes
8 ounces sliced pepperoni
8 ounces shredded mozzarella cheese
8 ounces shredded provolone cheese
8 ounces shredded fontina cheese
4 ounces grated Parmesan cheese
4 ounces Romano cheese
3 large Boboli® crusts (baked cheese pizza crusts)
Salt, pepper, oregano, garlic powder, basil, and crushed red pepper flakes

Directions:

Preheat oven to 425 degrees.

Place all the ingredients in separate bowls on kitchen counter. Set out Boboli crusts and allow guests to assemble their own pizzas, using sauces and toppings of their choice.

Place pizzas on baking screens.

Bake until the cheeses are melted and the crusts are crisp—about 15–20 minutes.

Yields: 3 pizza pies

TIP: For a crisper crust on your pizza—always use a pizza screen to bake the pizza in the oven!

PASTA WITH PESTO TOMATO CREAM

Ingredients:

1/2 pound pancetta
1/2 cup Classico® Traditional Basil Pesto
2 cups Classico® Tomato & Basil Pasta Sauce
1/2 cup chicken stock made from Wyler's® Chicken Bouillion
1/2 cup whipping cream
Freshly ground black pepper to taste

Pasta:

2 tablespoons olive oil
1 teaspoon salt
1 pound dried fusilli pasta
2 cups thawed frozen baby peas
Freshly grated Asiago cheese

Directions:

Sauce: Cook the pancetta in a medium skillet over medium heat, turning occasionally until crisp and brown. Drain on paper towels and crumble into bite-sized pieces. Combine the Classico Traditional Basil Pesto, the Classico Tomato & Basil Pasta Sauce, chicken stock, cream, and pepper in a medium saucepan over medium heat; and bring to a simmer. Whisk to blend the ingredients and cook for 5 minutes. Taste for seasoning.

Pasta: Add the oil and salt to large pot of boiling water. Add the pasta and cook over high heat until al dente. Drain well. Return the drained pasta back to the same pot. Add in the sauce and then carefully add in the pancetta and peas. Toss to combine. Taste for seasoning.

Serve immediately with the grated Asiago.

Serves: 4–6

TIP: Use a micro-plane to grate your Asiago cheese. The cheese should be very cold before grating and at room temperature to serve.

PUMPKIN RAVIOLI ALFREDO

Ingredients:
1/2 cup peeled hazelnuts
1/2 cup vegetable oil
1 pound fresh pumpkin
    ravioli
1 jar Classico® Four Cheese
    Alfredo Sauce
Large pinch grated nutmeg
Additional grated Parmesan
2 Amaretti cookies

Directions:
Preheat oven to 350 degrees.

Spread hazelnuts onto a baking tray. Toast hazelnuts in oven until light golden brown and fragrant, about 5–7 minutes. Allow to cool completely. Coarsely chop the cooled hazelnuts and set aside.

In a wide-bottomed pan with high sides, bring 2 quarts of salted water to a boil. Add the vegetable oil to prevent the ravioli from sticking to one another. Add ravioli and cook for 4 minutes or until they float to the top.

Using a strainer, carefully remove ravioli to a large platter and tent with foil to keep warm.

In a heavy sauce pot, heat the Classico Four Cheese Alfredo Sauce with the nutmeg. Pour the sauce over ravioli and sprinkle with toasted hazelnuts. Top the ravioli with additional grated Parmesan cheese to taste along with 2 Amaretti cookies that you have crumbled. Serve immediately.

Serves: 4

TIP: When toasting nuts, watch them very carefully, because an over-toasted nut will aquire a burnt and scorched taste.

E-Z GRILLED SALMON WITH TROPICAL FRUIT SALSA

Ingredients:

Tropical fruit salsa:
- 1/2 cup cantaloupe—diced
- 1/2 cup fresh pineapple chunks
- 1/2 cup fresh mango chunks
- 1/4 cup red bell pepper—diced
- 1/4 cup yellow bell pepper—diced
- 1/4 cup red onion—diced
- 2 tablespoons fresh-squeezed lime juice
- 2 tablespoons brown sugar
- 2 tablespoons fresh mint leaves—minced
- 1 teaspoon jalapeño pepper—minced
- Salt and pepper to taste

Salmon:
- 4–6-ounce salmon filets
- Jack Daniel's® Honey Teriyaki EZ Marinader® bag

Directions:

Salsa: Combine all of the salsa ingredients in a medium bowl. Cover and chill while grilling the salmon.

Open the EZ Marinader bag and place the 4 salmon filets in the bag. Zip the bag and place in the refrigerator to marinate for about 1 hour.

Preheat your gas grill to a medium-high heat. Oil the grill rack lightly and remove the salmon from the EZ Marinader bag. Discard the marinade and grill the salmon filets until cooked through, about 4 minutes per side, turning only once.

To serve: Place the salmon on the center of a serving plate and spoon the salsa all around the salmon.

Serves: 4

TIP: When working with jalapeño peppers, always wear thin plastic gloves. Never touch the peppers with your bare hands!

PORTOBELLO MUSHROOMS STUFFED WITH CRABMEAT

Ingredients:

1 pound jumbo lump crabmeat—picked over for cartilage
1 egg
1 tablespoon mayonnaise
1 teaspoon Heinz® Spicy Brown Mustard
12 Saltine crackers
1 tablespoon Old Bay® Seasoning
1 teaspoon Heinz® Worcestershire Sauce (or to taste)
4 large Portobello mushrooms—stems removed—cut into
    fluted rounds using a 2-1/2-inch fluted cookie cutter
2 teaspoons unsalted butter
Paprika for sprinkling
Lemon slices / confit of chopped tomatoes and green onions

Directions:

Place the crabmeat into a medium bowl. In a separate bowl, combine egg, mayonnaise, mustard, crackers, Old Bay Seasoning, and Worcestershire Sauce. Mix well. Gently fold mixture into the crabmeat.

Cut the portobello mushrooms into perfect fluted rounds using the cookie cutter.

PORTOBELLO MUSHROOMS STUFFED WITH CRABMEAT

Place the crab mixture equally on top of each portobello mushroom and mound to fit using your hands. Top each center of the stuffing with 1/4 teaspoon of butter. Refrigerate for 2 hours.

Preheat oven to 380 degrees. Bake for 15 minutes and then place under the broiler for 2 minutes. Sprinkle with paprika. Garnish with lemon, confit of tomatoes, and green onions.

Yields: 4 servings

TIP: For a quick way to "see" the cartilage in crabmeat, put the crabmeat on a parchment-lined baking pan in the oven for a few minutes at 250 degrees. The cartilage will turn white and, thus, be very visible to the naked eye!

CRAB BURGER PO' BOYS

Ingredients:

Mustard mayonnaise:
1/4 cup mayonnaise
4 tablespoons finely chopped Heinz® Sweet Pickles
2 tablespoons drained capers
2 tablespoons Dijon mustard

Crab burgers:
1/4 cup minced green onion
1/4 cup minced green bell pepper
2 tablespoons unsalted butter
1/2 pound lump crabmeat—picked over
1/4 cup thinly sliced scallion greens
4 tablespoons mayonnaise
2 tablespoons lightly beaten egg
1/2 cup + 1 tablespoon fine dry breadcrumbs
Generous dash of Heinz® Worcestershire Sauce
Cayenne to taste
Vegetable oil for frying
2 5-inch lengths crisp French baguette—split
Leaf lettuce
Ore-Ida® Zesty Fries™ with Heinz® Ketchup Kick'rs®

CRAB BURGER PO' BOYS

Directions:

Mayonnaise: Whisk together the mayonnaise ingredients and reserve.

Crab burgers: In a small, heavy skillet, cook the onion and bell pepper in butter over moderately low heat, stirring occasionally, until softened. In a bowl, stir together onion mixture, crabmeat, scallions, mayonnaise, egg, 1 tablespoon breadcrumbs, Worcestershire Sauce, cayenne, and salt to taste. Put remaining breadcrumbs in a small bowl. Form 1/4 of the crab mixture into a 3-inch patty and coat it with the breadcrumbs. Make three more patties and place them on a parchment-lined baking pan. Chill them well before frying.

In a 10-inch, nonstick skillet, heat 1/4-inch of vegetable oil over moderately high heat until hot, but not smoking, and fry patties until golden and cooked through, about 2-1/2 minutes on each side, transferring to paper towels to drain.

Spread bread with reserved mustard mayonnaise and sandwich crab burgers and leaf lettuce between bread.

Makes 2 sandwiches

TIP: For a healthier version of this recipe, broil the crab cakes instead of frying them.

GRILLED SALMON WITH RANIA'S CHERRY COLA BARBECUE SAUCE

Ingredients:
3/4 cup cherry cola barbecue sauce
6 5-ounce salmon filets

Cherry cola barbecue sauce:
2 tablespoons extra virgin olive oil
1 large yellow onion—chopped
4 cloves of garlic—minced
8 cups cherry cola
2 cups Heinz® Ketchup
1 cup Heinz® Apple Cider Vinegar
1 tablespoon chopped chipotle chile
2 teaspoons sweet paprika
2 teaspoons fresh-ground black pepper
1 teaspoon kosher salt

Directions:
Cherry cola barbecue sauce: Heat the olive oil in a large skillet over medium heat. Add the onion and cook for 10 minutes. Add the garlic and cook for another minute or two. Add the cherry cola and bring to a boil. Cook this mixture for 45 minutes, until reduced to one-quarter of the amount. Stir in the ketchup, vinegar, chipotle, paprika, pepper, and salt. Cook for 15 minutes or until thick. This will keep in an airtight container in the refrigerator for up to 6 weeks.

GRILLED SALMON WITH RANIA'S CHERRY COLA BARBECUE SAUCE

Prepare the barbecue sauce ahead. Heat your grill to a high heat. Spray the grate with nonstick spray to prevent the salmon from sticking. You may also grill your salmon on a nonstick (preheated) stove top grill pan.

Grill the salmon for about 3–4 minutes per side, basting with the cherry cola barbecue sauce during the grilling process. Be careful not to overcook the salmon, or it will dry out. Just before serving the grilled salmon, brush on more of the sauce.

Serves 6

TIP: If your grill has a lid, close it to allow smoke to add additional flavor.

LEMON RISOTTO WITH JUMBO SHRIMP

Ingredients:

Risotto:
2 tablespoons + 2 teaspoons unsalted butter
2 tablespoons olive oil
1/4 cup minced onion
2 teaspoons grated lemon rind
1-1/2 cups arborio rice (uncooked)
4-1/2 cups hot chicken stock made from Wyler's® Bouillon
1/4 cup + 2 teaspoons lemon juice
1 teaspoon freshly chopped thyme leaves

Shrimp and assembly:
12 jumbo shrimp—in the shell
3 tablespoons unsalted butter—melted
Coarse salt and freshly ground black pepper
1/4 cup finely minced fresh chives

Directions:

Risotto: In a large, heavy saucepan over medium-low heat, melt 2 tablespoons of butter with 2 tablespoons olive oil. Add onion and lemon rind and sauté slowly for 3 minutes. Add rice and stir to coat with oil. Turn heat up to high and cook the rice, stirring for 30 seconds. Immediately add 1/2 cup of the stock. Reduce the heat to medium-low and stir until stock is absorbed. Add more stock, 1/2 cup at a time, stirring constantly and adding more only when previous portion of stock has been absorbed. When all stock is absorbed (after about 20–25 minutes) stir in 1/4 cup of the lemon juice. The rice should be tender. Stir in thyme leaves and remaining butter. Season to taste (if needed) with salt and pepper. Add remaining lemon juice.

LEMON RISOTTO WITH JUMBO SHRIMP

Shrimp and assembly: Preheat broiler. Using a sharp chef's knife, cut through the shells to split the shrimp in half lengthwise. Arrange them, cut side up, in a shallow broiling pan. Brush them with melted butter and season with salt and pepper. Broil for 3–4 minutes, or until lightly browned and opaque in the center. Stir the chives into the risotto. Taste and season with salt and pepper. Spoon the risotto onto warmed plates and garnish each serving with shrimp.

Serves: 6

TIP: For perfect risotto, always heat the chicken stock to a simmer and keep it simmering over a low heat while adding it to the risotto.

BARBECUED CHICKEN QUESADILLA WITH AVOCADO SALSA

Ingredients:

1 cup Jack Daniel's® Original No. 7 Recipe™ Barbecue Sauce
2 chicken breasts—boneless and skinless
3 6-inch flour tortillas
1/4 cup grated Monterey Jack cheese
1/4 cup grated white cheddar cheese
Salt and pepper to taste

Avocado salsa:

1 ripe avocado—coarsely chopped
1 tablespoon finely chopped red onion
1 tablespoon minced jalapeño
2 tablespoons fresh lime juice
Salt and pepper to taste

Directions:

Prepare Jack Daniel's Barbecue Sauce to medium-high heat. Brush the chicken with the barbecue sauce and season to taste with salt and pepper. Grill the chicken for about 4 minutes per side or until done. When the chicken is cool enough to handle, slice it and set it aside. Place 2 tortillas on an ungreased baking sheet. Spread 1/2 of the cheeses and the chicken on each tortilla and season to taste with salt and pepper. Stack the 2 layers, cover with the remaining tortilla. Brush the tortilla lightly with olive oil. Grill for 3 minutes on each side or until the tortillas are crisp and the cheese is melted.

Cut into quarters and serve hot, garnished with the avocado salsa.

To make the salsa:

Combine all of the avocado salsa ingredients together in a bowl and season with salt and pepper.

Serves: 4 as an appetizer

TIP: Always add lemon or lime juice to any recipe with avocado. This will help prevent the avocado from turning brown in the recipe.

BARBECUED CHICKEN QUESADILLA WITH AVOCADO SALSA

FRANCO'S 1972 COCKTAIL MEATBALLS

Ingredients:

2 pounds lean ground beef
4 tablespoons unsalted butter
1 medium onion—chopped
2 eggs—lightly beaten
4 slices whole-wheat
    bread— toasted and
    crumbled (crusts
    removed)
1-1/2 cups tomato sauce

Salt and pepper to taste
1/2 cup chopped fresh
    parsley
All-purpose flour
Vegetable oil for frying

Sauce:

1 12-ounce bottle Heinz® Chili Sauce
1 10-ounce jar grape jelly

FRANCO'S 1972 COCKTAIL MEATBALLS

Directions:

Meatballs: Place the ground beef in a mixing bowl and set aside.

Melt the butter in a medium heavy skillet and sauté the onion until it is completely cooked through and almost golden in color.

Add the cooked onion to the ground beef along with the eggs, crumbled bread, tomato sauce, salt and pepper to taste, and parsley. Gently mix the meatball mixture with your hands until well combined.

Form meatballs the size of a large walnut and set on a baking sheet. Heat enough vegetable oil in a large heavy skillet about 1/2-inch deep. Dust the meatballs in the flour and fry them just until they are golden brown and cooked through—turning once. Remove the meatballs from the oil and drain them on paper towels.

Sauce: Combine the chili sauce and grape jelly in a medium pot, and heat until bubbling. Add the meatballs to the sauce and gently heat through. Put the cocktail meatballs in a fondue pot and serve with cocktail forks.

Serves: 8–10

TIP: After frying the first batch of meatballs, discard the oil and wash the pan. Start the next batch with clean oil. The result is a much lighter-tasting meatball, without the heavy oily taste.

SMASHIN' BASHIN' BEAN SOUP

Ingredients:

1/4 cup olive oil

2 large cloves garlic—peeled and chopped

1 Spanish onion—peeled and chopped

1 zucchini (about 12 ounces) cut into 1/2-inch dice (about 2-1/2 cups diced)

1 yellow bell pepper—stemmed, seeded and cut into 1/2-inch dice

1 red bell pepper—stemmed, seeded, and cut into 1/2-inch dice

1 tablespoon chopped fresh basil

1/2 teaspoon dried thyme

Kosher salt to taste

4 cups vegetable stock made from Wyler's® Vegetable Bouillon

SMASHIN' BASHIN' BEAN SOUP

1 pound canned plum tomatoes—chopped, with their juice

1/3 cup pitted Kalamata olives

2 cans (16 ounces each) Heinz® Vegetarian Beans, rinsed and drained

4 ounces fresh spinach leaves—trimmed, washed and coarsely chopped

Freshly ground black pepper to taste

For garnish:
Parmesan croutons
Classico Creations® Pesto

Directions:

Heat the oil in a large stock pot over medium heat. Add the garlic and onion, and sauté until the onion is very tender and just beginning to brown, about 10 minutes. Add the zucchini, bell peppers, basil, thyme, and 1/2 teaspoon salt. Sauté another 5 minutes.

Stir in the Wyler's Vegetable stock, canned tomatoes with their juice, and olives. Bring to a boil, reduce the heat, partially cover and simmer gently for 25–30 minutes.

Add the Heinz Vegetarian Beans and spinach, and cook over medium heat just until the beans have warmed and the spinach has wilted, about 5 minutes. Season to taste with salt and pepper, and add a bit more stock for a thinner soup—if desired.

Garnish with croutons and Classico Creations Pesto.

Serves: 12

TIP: Always sauté garlic and onions first in a little olive oil before proceeding with your favorite recipe for soup or sauces, as the end result will taste sweeter and milder.

SEASONED CHICKEN BURGERS

Ingredients:
1-1/2 cups dried herb-
seasoned stuffing cubes
1 pound ground chicken
(boneless, skinless
breasts)
1/2 cup finely chopped
celery
1/2 cup finely chopped
onion
2 egg yolks
Salt and black pepper
to taste

Topping:
1/2 cup Heinz® Chili Sauce
1/2 cup canned whole-berry
cranberry sauce
Vegetable oil
4 whole-wheat hamburger
buns

Directions:
Process the stuffing cubes in
the bowl of food processor
until fine crumbs form.
Transfer 1/2 of the crumbs
into a mixing bowl.

Mix in the chicken, celery,
onions, egg yolks, salt, and
pepper.

Blend ingredients together
and form into 4-1/2-inch-
thick patties.

Place remaining crumbs in
a shallow pan and coat the
patties well.

Combine the chili sauce
with the cranberry sauce in
another bowl and set aside.

If grilling the burgers—
brush the grill with some
of the vegetable oil so that
they won't stick during the
grilling process. If broiling
the burgers, preheat the
broiler. Grill or broil the
burgers until cooked through
—about 7 minutes per side.

Serve on the whole-wheat
buns with the chili-cranberry
sauce topping the burgers.

Serves: 4

TIP: For a different twist on
this recipe, try substituting
ground turkey for the
chicken.

SEASONED CHICKEN BURGERS

CHICKEN BREASTS WITH CHIMICHURRI SAUCE

57 SPECIAL TAILGATING RECIPES
AND COOKING TIPS

CHICKEN BREASTS WITH CHIMICHURRI SAUCE

Ingredients:

Chimichurri sauce:

10 garlic cloves—peeled
1 bunch flat-leaf parsley—
    stemmed
3/4 cup olive oil
1/4 cup Heinz® Balsamic
    Vinegar
1/4 cup chicken stock made
    from Wyler's® Bouillon
3/4 teaspoon dried oregano
3/4 teaspoon dried basil
3/4 teaspoon red pepper
    flakes
Salt and freshly ground black
    pepper to taste

Marinade:

3 tablespoons chimichurri
    sauce
2 tablespoons olive oil
3 whole chicken breasts—
    halved, boned, flattened

Directions:

To make the sauce: In a food processor fitted with the metal blade, purée the garlic. Add the parsley and process until finely chopped. Add the oil, vinegar, stock, and seasonings. Process to blend. Taste and adjust the seasonings.

It should be very flavorful and spicy.

In a small bowl, combine all the marinade ingredients and stir until smooth. Put the chicken breasts in a resealable plastic bag and pour in the marinade. Turn the chicken in the bag to coat it evenly. Close the bag and refrigerate for at least 30 minutes or up to 4 hours.

Heat your grill to a medium-high heat or heat a stove top nonstick grill pan. Remove the chicken from the marinade and grill for about 6–7 minutes on each side or until the chicken is cooked through.

Place on a large platter and serve with sauce on the side.

Serves: 4–6

TIP: Use a salad spinner to wash the parsley. The salad spinner not only cleans the parsley well, it also removes all of the excess water.

GRILLED RIB-EYE STEAK WITH TENNESSEE-STYLE MOP SAUCE

Ingredients:
Sauce:
2 12-ounce cans of beer
6 ounces Heinz® Spicy
    Brown Mustard
8 ounces Heinz®
    Worcestershire Sauce
16 ounces Jack Daniel's®
    Hickory Mesquite
    Barbecue Sauce
4 ounces honey
Pinch of hot chile flakes
4 ounces Heinz® Red Wine
    Vinegar
1 large white onion—
    chopped
2 lemons—sliced

6 rib-eye steaks—about
    8–10 ounces each
Ore-Ida® Extra Crispy Fries
Heinz® Organic Ketchup

Directions:
For the sauce: Combine all the sauce ingredients in a large pot. Bring to a boil, reduce heat and cook on a medium heat until all the ingredients are blended and the sauce begins to thicken, about 30–40 minutes.

Preheat the grill to a medium-high heat.

Mop the steaks with the sauce and grill them to the desired degree of doneness.

Warm the remaining sauce and serve it on the side.

Serves: 6

TIP: When buying steaks, choose thicker cuts that have a good amount of marbled fat, because marbling results in a much tastier steak.

GRILLED RIB-EYE STEAK WITH TENNESSEE-STYLE MOP SAUCE

JACK DANIEL'S® MARINATED FLANK STEAK WITH HONEY CHILI SAUCE

57 SPECIAL TAILGATING RECIPES
AND COOKING TIPS

JACK DANIEL'S MARINATED FLANK STEAK WITH HONEY CHILI SAUCE

Ingredients:
2-1/2 pounds flank steak

Marinade:
1 12-ounce bag Jack Daniel's® Mesquite EZ Marinader® bag

Sauce:
1/4 cup honey
2 tablespoons peanut oil
4 canned jalapeño peppers
2 tablespoons Heinz® Balsamic Vinegar
2 tablespoons Heinz® Spicy Brown Mustard
1/2 cup freshly squeezed lime juice
2 cloves garlic
1 teaspoon ground cumin
2 tablespoons chopped cilantro
Salt and fresh cracked black pepper to taste

Directions:
Place the steak in the marinade bag and marinate according to the package directions.

To make the sauce: Combine the honey, peanut oil, peppers, vinegar, mustard, lime juice, garlic, and cumin; and purée in the bowl of a food processor. Stir in the chopped cilantro and season with salt and pepper to taste.

To grill the steak: Remove the steak from the EZ Marinader bag and discard the bag with the marinade. Grill the steak over high heat until steak reaches your cooked preference.

Remove steak from the grill and let it rest for 5 minutes. Slice the steak against the grain and serve with the sauce.

Serves: 6

TIP: When ready to grill the flank steak, score it on the diagonal and repeat the process on the opposite diagonal to create a "crisscross" pattern on the meat. This allows for more even cooking.

BARBECUED SPARERIBS WITH RED-HOT SAUCE

Ingredients:

3 cups Heinz® Chili Sauce
2/3 cup apple jelly
4 tablespoons Heinz® Apple
    Cider Vinegar
2 tablespoons dry mustard
1/4 cup Heinz®
    Worcestershire Sauce
1 tablespoon TABASCO®
    (or to taste)
1/2 teaspoon cayenne
    pepper (or to taste)
5 pounds baby back
    spareribs—cut into
    4-rib sections
Salt to taste

Directions:

Sauce: Bring first seven ingredients to boil in heavy saucepan over medium heat, stirring occasionally. Reduce heat and simmer for a few minutes. Cool.

Season the ribs with salt. Roast them in a preheated, 350-degree oven on a rack. Do not cover the ribs.

Turn them once and cook them until they are tender, almost completely cooked, about 45–60 minutes.

When ready to serve— preheat your grill to a medium-high heat. Put the rib rack halves on the grill and brush them with the sauce. Grill them until they are well-glazed and browned, and completely cooked.

Transfer the ribs to a large serving platter and pass remaining sauce separately.

Serves: 4–6

TIP: After you take the ribs out of the oven, tent them with foil to allow the juices to collect and keep the ribs good and moist.

BARBECUED SPARERIBS WITH RED-HOT SAUCE

PULLED PORK WITH ROOT BEER BBQ SAUCE

Ingredients:

1 8-pound pork shoulder
Salt and pepper
2 heads garlic cloves—
    separated and peeled

Root beer BBQ sauce:

Reduce 1 2-liter bottle root
    beer to 1 cup
1-1/2 cups Heinz® Apple
    Cider Vinegar
1/2 cup Heinz® Ketchup
1/2 cup Heinz® Yellow
    Mustard
2 tablespoons lemon juice
1 tablespoon Heinz®
    Worcestershire Sauce
1 tablespoon TABASCO®
1 teaspoon kosher salt
1 teaspoon black pepper

To finish sauce:

2 tablespoons cold, unsalted
    butter

PULLED PORK WITH ROOT BEER BBQ SAUCE

Directions:

Preheat oven to 225 degrees.

Place the pork shoulder, fat side up, in a large roasting pan and season well with salt and pepper to taste. Toss 2 heads of garlic cloves that have been peeled, but leave cloves whole around the pork. Cover well with heavy-duty aluminum foil. Slow-cook in the oven until tender and falling apart, and the internal temperature reaches 160 degrees. This should take about 6 to 8 hours. Remove from the oven and let the pork rest for 20 to 30 minutes. With two forks, pull apart the meat into small chunks. Toss with the root beer BBQ sauce and serve.

Root beer BBQ sauce:
Reduce the root beer to 1 cup over medium heat in a large saucepan—this takes about 1 hour.

Add the vinegar, ketchup, mustard, lemon juice, worcestershire sauce, tabasco, salt, and pepper. Stir well and simmer for 20 minutes. Finish the sauce by whisking in the cold butter for extra body and flavor.

Serves: 6–8

TIP: Never use diet root beer in this recipe! The sugar in the root beer is critical to the success of the recipe.

PEPPERED VODKA SAUCE WITH PENNE PASTA

Ingredients:

2 tablespoons olive oil
1/2 cup green onions—
   chopped
1 tablespoon garlic—
   chopped
1/4 pound sliced prosciutto

1 jar Classico® Vodka Pasta
   Sauce
5 ripe plum tomatoes
Fresh-cracked black pepper to
   taste
1 10-ounce box frozen peas
   —thawed
1 small bunch fresh basil—
   chopped

1 pound penne pasta—
   cooked al dente
1/2 cup grated cheese for
   topping pasta

Directions:

In a medium saucepan, heat the olive oil and sauté onion until almost caramelized. Add in the garlic and proscuitto. Add in the Classico Vodka Pasta Sauce and chopped tomatoes. Season to taste with fresh-cracked black pepper. Bring to a simmer and cook for 1 minute. Add the peas and the basil.

Toss with pasta and top with grated cheese

Serves: 4

TIP: When chopping garlic, sprinkle a little salt so the pieces won't stick to your knife or cutting board.

PEPPERED VODKA SAUCE WITH PENNE PASTA

GRILLED TUNA WITH CHILI SALSA

57 SPECIAL TAILGATING RECIPES
AND COOKING TIPS

GRILLED TUNA WITH CHILI SALSA

Ingredients:
6 5-ounce fresh tuna filets
3 tablespoons olive oil
4 tablespoons lemon juice
Fresh garlic
Salt and pepper to taste

Chili salsa:
1 bottle (12 ounces) Heinz® Chili Sauce
1/2 cup green bell pepper—finely chopped
1/2 cup yellow bell pepper—finely chopped
1/2 cup onion—finely chopped
2 teaspoons cilantro—finely chopped

Directions:
Place the tuna filets in a shallow pan. Make a marinade with the 3 tablespoons olive oil, 4 tablespoons lemon juice, and enough minced fresh garlic, salt and pepper to taste. Cover and refrigerate for at least 30 minutes.

In a medium bowl, combine all salsa ingredients.

When ready to serve, preheat grill to medium-high heat. Grill the tuna on both sides until just cooked through. Do not overcook or it will dry out. I like mine pink on the inside.

To serve: Place a tuna filet on a plate and top with the chili salsa.

Garnish with fresh cilantro.

Serves: 6

TIP: For a really spicy chili salsa, use Heinz® Zesty Chili Sauce instead of Heinz Chili Sauce.

SHRIMP CREOLE

Ingredients:

6 tablespoons butter
I cup onions—julienned
I cup green pepper—
    julienned
2 stalks celery—in julienne
    strips
2 cloves garlic—chopped
I bay leaf
2 tablespoons paprika
2 cups tomatoes—diced
1/2 cup Heinz® Ketchup
4 teaspoons Heinz®
    Worcestershire Sauce
2 tablespoons TABASCO®
1-1/2 tablespoons cornstarch
1/2 cup water
3 pounds shrimp—peeled
    and deveined

Directions:

Melt 2 tablespoons butter
in a sauté pan and sauté
onion, green pepper, celery,
garlic, and bay leaf for a few
minutes. Add paprika,
tomatoes and Heinz
Ketchup. Stir well. Add
Heinz Worcestershire Sauce
and TABASCO, and simmer
until volume is reduced by
one-fourth and the
vegetables are soft. Stir into
the sauce for about 2 minutes
to cook the cornstarch.

Sauté the shrimp in the
remaining butter until pink
and tender, about 5 minutes,
stirring constantly. Pour
sauce over shrimp and toss
to coat well.

Serve with fluffy cooked rice.

Serves: 6–8

TIP: Your can use canned
diced tomatoes in this recipe
for a quick shortcut.

SHRIMP CREOLE

GRAND PRIZE WINNER—

57 SPECIAL TAILGATING RECIPES
AND COOKING TIPS

TANGY SPORTSMAN MUSHROOMS

Ingredients:
- 2 pounds large mushrooms
- 4 tablespoons butter
- 1/4 cup Ore-Ida® Chopped Onions
- 1/2-pound ground pork sausage
- 1 4-ounce package cream cheese—softened
- 2/3 cup Jack Daniel's® Original No. 7 Recipe™ Barbecue Sauce
- 4 tablespoons Heinz® 57 Sauce
- 1/4 cup grated Parmesan cheese

Directions:
Preheat oven to 350 degrees.

Remove stems from the mushrooms, leaving the caps intact.

Chop the stems.

In a medium saucepan, melt the butter. Then lightly brush the mushroom caps with melted butter.

In the remaining butter, cook and stir the sausage, chopped mushroom stems, and onions until tender and the sausage is fully cooked.

Gradually mix the cream cheese, Jack Daniel's Barbecue Sauce and Heinz 57 Sauce into the saucepan. Continue stirring until smooth. Heat until warm.

Stuff the mushroom caps with the sausage-cream cheese mixture and sprinkle the stuffed caps with Parmesan cheese.

In a shallow pan, bake the caps at 350 degrees for 8–12 minutes or until hot.

Recipe by Chris Wyerchowski of Venice, Florida.

HEINZ KETCHUP'S LOVE APPLE PIE

Ingredients:
1/3 cup Heinz® Ketchup
2 teaspoon lemon juice
6 cups tart cooking apples—peeled and sliced (about 2 lbs.)
2/3 cup all-purpose flour
1/3 cup granulated sugar
1 teaspoon cinnamon
1/3 cup unsalted butter or margarine, softened
1 unbaked 9-inch pie shell

Directions:
Blend Heinz Ketchup and lemon juice; combine with apples. (Note: If apples are very tart, add 1 to 2 tablespoons sugar to ketchup mixture.)

For topping: Combine flour, sugar and cinnamon; cut in butter until thoroughly mixed. Fill pie shell with apples; sprinkle topping over apples. Bake in 425-degrees oven, 40–45 minutes or until apples are cooked. Serve warm with ice cream, if desired.

Makes one 9-inch pie

TIP: Don't cut apple pieces too thin when you are using fresh apples. Larger chunks will hold together and have more apple flavor.

HEINZ KETCHUP'S
LOVE APPLE PIE

57 SPECIAL TAILGATING RECIPES
AND COOKING TIPS

195

HEINZ KETCHUP'S TIC-TAC-TOE COOKIES

Ingredients:
1-1/2 cups sifted all-purpose flour
1/2 teaspoon baking soda
1/2 teaspoon salt
1/2 cup butter or margarine—softened
1/2 cup sugar
1/2 cup firmly packed brown sugar
3/4 cup chunky or creamy peanut butter
1/4 cup Heinz® Ketchup
1 egg

Directions:
Sift together flour, baking soda and salt. In another bowl, cream together butter and next three ingredients until light and fluffy. Add ketchup and egg; mix well. Thoroughly blend flour mixture into peanut butter mixture. Drop teaspoonfuls onto greased baking sheets. With fork in flour, press cookie flat, making impression in two directions. Bake in preheated, 375-degree oven for 8–10 minutes (10 minutes on an insulated cookie sheet and 8 minutes on a regular nonstick sheet) or until golden brown. Cool on wire rack.

Makes 4-1/2–5 dozen

RECIPE INDEX

RECIPE INDEX

RECIPE INDEX

RECIPE INDEX

MEASUREMENTS AND EQUIVALENTS

Measurements

Dash	=	less than 1/8 teaspoon
1 tablespoon	=	3 teaspoons
2 tablespoons	=	1 ounce
4 tablespoons	=	1/4 cup
5-1/3 tablespoons	=	1/3 cup
8 tablespoons	=	1/2 cup
16 tablespoons	=	1 cup
8 fluid ounces	=	1 cup
16 fluid ounces	=	1 pound
2 cups	=	1 pound / 1 pint
2 pints	=	1 quart / 4 cups
4 quarts	=	1 gallon

Metric Conversion Volume

1 teaspoon	=	5 milliliters
1 tablespoon	=	15 milliliters
2 tablespoons	=	30 milliliters
1 cup	=	240 milliliters
1 pint	=	480 milliliters
1 quart	=	960 milliliters

Weight

1 ounce	=	28 grams
1 pound	=	454 grams
2.2 pounds	=	1 kilogram (1,000 grams)

THE WESTERN PENNSYLVANIA SPORTS MUSEUM

Few cities enjoy the tremendous sports history that Pittsburgh can boast. It's only fitting that a city with such legendary sports heroes and teams now has a place to honor those Pittsburghers who became champions and the champions who became Pittsburghers.

The Western Pennsylvania Sports Museum, located in the new Smithsonian wing of the Senator John Heinz Pittsburgh Regional History Center, shares the long, rich history of sports in our region.

This interactive, 20,000-square-foot exhibit features recreated environments, interactive elements and kiosks, video presentations, images, and more. Hundreds of artifacts such as game-worn uniforms, one-of-a-kind trophies and sports equipment—artifacts related to fan involvement and our rich tradition of classic sports stadiums—bring you face-to-face with the history of sports in western Pennsylvania.

Your purchase of this book will help us keep the memories alive.

CHARLES REICHBLUM

Author

Charles Reichblum, nicknamed "Dr. Knowledge" by radio talk show hosts around the country, has built one of the largest collections in the world of fascinating facts and stories that serve as a source for his *Knowledge in a Nutshell®* books, the *Dr. Knowledge Presents Strange and Fascinating Facts* books, the questions-and-answers inside *The Edible Game A Smart Cookie™*, *The Dr. Knowledge Show* broadcast on Pittsburgh's 1020 KDKA radio and the new *Heinz Field Touchdowns to Tailgating.*

As to what makes his books and radio show so appealing, "The Doctor" says it's the "I bet-you-didn't-know spirit in all of us who like to stump our friends—and savor the facts and interesting stories behind them for ourselves."

Reichblum is married with two sons, two daughters-in-law, and four grandchildren.

Charles Reichblum is one of the most stimulating and entertaining guests on my radio program. Listeners love his wit and knowledge. Not only is it fun, but we learn a lot, too."

—JORDAN RICH, WBZ, BOSTON

RANIA L. HARRIS

Certified Chef & Owner—
Rania's Catering, Mt. Lebanon, PA

Rania Harris is a certified chef, event coordinator, cooking school teacher, and local television and radio talent who began her catering business twenty-eight years ago from her Mt. Lebanon kitchen. Her goal was to cater "just a few" parties a year—to satisfy her love for cooking and entertaining. One party led to another and her business grew into a full-scale catering operation, as well as a gourmet take-out shop, café, cooking school, and pastry shop.

Harris's natural sense of food presentation was enhanced by her studies with Master Pastry Chef Gunther Heiland and the Culinary Institute's Chef Timothy Ryan (formerly of La Normande). Her culinary career has included catering for Presidential candidates, senators, governors, and several well-known Hollywood personalities. Throughout the years, her philosophy has remained simple and consistent: Treat each one of her clients and students as though they were guests in her own home—and never hold back on a recipe request!

Harris has served as a Heinz media spokesperson, including at the Heinz Tailgatin' Station at Heinz Field. For eight years, Harris had a regular cooking segment on WTAE-TV's weekend news. She has taught cooking segments on *Pittsburgh's Talking, Evening Magazine, Hello Pittsburgh,* and *Pittsburgh Today.* She can now be seen on KDKA-TV2.

Besides being heavily involved with the local culinary community, Harris was featured nationally in *Bon Appétit* (April 1985) as "an outstanding cooking school teacher."